Randall Jarrell: A Bibliography

RANDALL JARRELL
A BIBLIOGRAPHY

COMPILED BY
CHARLES M. ADAMS

CHAPEL HILL
The University of North Carolina Press
1958

© Copyright, 1958, by
The University of North Carolina Press

Manufactured in the United States of America

Contents

	Preface	7
	Introduction by Robert Humphrey	11
I	Books by Randall Jarrell	15
	1. *Blood for a Stranger*, 1942	
	2. *Little Friend, Little Friend*, 1945	
	3. *Losses*, 1948	
	4. *The Seven-League Crutches*, 1951	
	5. *Poetry and the Age*, 1953	
	6. *Pictures from an Institution*, 1954	
	7. *Selected Poems*, 1955	
II	Collections Indexed for Contributions by Randall Jarrell: Arranged by Title of Collections	28
III	Poems by Randall Jarrell: An Index by Title and First Line When No Title	34
IV	Prose by Randall Jarrell: An Index by Title	58
V	Book Reviews by Randall Jarrell: Arranged Chronologically	64
VI	Translations by Randall Jarrell: Arranged by Author	70
VII	Randall Jarrell: Brief Biographical Notes, Publications, Literary Prizes, and Appointments	71

Preface

THE bibliography of Randall Jarrell is based on a special collection of his writing in the Library of the Woman's College of the University of North Carolina. The Library has all the first editions of his books and a number of the later printings. Mr. Jarrell has presented the Library with many original manuscripts of his writings. Location of these is noted in Parts III, IV, V, and VI by means of an asterisk (*) following the title. There are also assorted incomplete poetry and prose manuscripts not located. Most of the periodicals and anthologies listed are in the Woman's College Library but a few were examined at the New York Public Library, the Duke University Library, the Library at the University of North Carolina at Chapel Hill, or at the Library of Congress. An attempt has been made to include all published material through 1957.

The bibliography is divided into six parts as follows:

Part I *Books by Randall Jarrell*
    The books are arranged by the date of the first edition.
Part II *Collections Indexed for Contributions by Randall Jarrell*
    These collections are arranged alphabetically by title.
Part III *Poems by Randall Jarrell*
    Each poem is listed alphabetically by title with a chronological arrangement for its publication.
Part IV *Prose by Randall Jarrell*
    Each prose piece is listed alphabetically by title with a chronological arrangement for its publication.
Part V *Book Reviews by Randall Jarrell*
    The reviews are listed by date of publication. Some reviews are essays or articles and so treated in later publications. In such cases these review articles are treated as prose pieces under Part IV with cross references where it seems necessary.

PREFACE

Part VI *Translations by Randall Jarrell*
These are arranged alphabetically by author with cross references from the poems in Part III.

A section of articles about Randall Jarrell and his writing was compiled but as most of these are readily available in published indexes to periodicals, it did not seem necessary to include them here. Sister M. Bernetta Quinn lists a selection of these in her bibliography on the chapter devoted to Randall Jarrell in *The Metamorphic Tradition in Modern Poetry* (New Brunswick, N. J.: Rutgers University Press, 1955), pp. 258–259.

According to his own statement Randall Jarrell did not have any poetry published in undergraduate publications. He had already had his first poems published in the *American Review* for May 1934. He was, however, editor of the *Vanderbilt Masquerader* for 1934–35. Through the courtesy of Dr. A. F. Kuhlman, Director of the Joint University Libraries, photostat copies of these editorials and of one signed article have been obtained for the collection in Woman's College Library. A microfilm copy of his Master's thesis, 'Implicit Generalizations in Housman', June 1939, was also obtained. It was decided not to include his work in undergraduate publications in this bibliography.

Part I, devoted to his books, is arranged by date of the first edition of each title. There are seven titles in all; foreign and later editions are listed as sub-entries under the original title. For each edition a full bibliographic description was made using quasi-facsimile rules for descriptions of the title page, and conventional symbols, such as square brackets for assumed information, descriptions of ornaments, devices, etc., and line-endings to indicate spacing on the page. A full collation was made for each book and checked with the signatures. Notes and full contents are given for the first edition and variances for later editions are noted.

For Parts II through VI a brief form of description was used. The purpose of these sections was to index each poem or prose writing and to list in chronological order its publication in his books, in collections, anthologies and in periodicals. Reading of his poems for phonographic recordings was also included. A number of his poems and his prose pieces were changed slightly or rewritten for later publication. A number of these changes Mr. Jarrell has noted in the introductions to his books. These notes are included in the descriptions in Part I. A few of the completely rewritten versions of his poems have been noted in the indexes in the later parts, but a complete textual study of changes in later printings has not been made. One must be careful in assuming that later printings of a work are exactly as earlier printings even if not so noted.

Thanks are due to many friends and colleagues: to Robert Humphrey, Assistant Professor of English at the Woman's College, who not only contributed the Introduction but also contributed many suggestions as to notes; to Francis Laine, Associate Professor of Classics, who contributed a number of pieces to the collection and called a number of obscure items to my attention; to Gerald McDonald, of The New York Public Library, who made valuable suggestions as to the form of the bibliography and gifts to the collection; to Barron Franz, Chief of the Periodical Division of The New York Public Library, for help in locating some difficult references; to Thomas Lash of *The New York Times* for aid in locating poetry that appeared in that paper; to Elizabeth Sampson, Head Cataloger at the Woman's College Library, for her patient checking and reading of the manuscript, and finally to Randall Jarrell himself and to his wife, without whose personal help this bibliography could not have been as complete nor as enjoyable a project on which to work. A brief chronology of positions held by Randall Jarrell, of his books, awards, and appointments is appended to the bibliography. The Library of the Woman's College of the University of North Carolina considers it a privilege to be the repository for the manuscript material Mr. Jarrell has presented to it. Some financial assistance in the preparation of this bibliography was given by the Research Council of the Woman's College. The special collection of books, manuscripts, and related materials will be sources for future students of his work.

Woman's College
University of North Carolina
January 1958

CHARLES M. ADAMS, *Librarian*

Introduction

THE luxury of writing a foreword to a poet's bibliography allows us to be concerned briefly with the human and poetic nature of his achievement. With Randall Jarrell's bibliography, we are almost certain to suggest, in addition, a mild sort of *apologia*, for it was only four or five years ago that we spoke of him as 'one of the promising young writers'. The careful, exhaustive bibliography below suggests that Jarrell might be, after all, the most important poet of his generation; and, if he is, there is the obvious question: Why has Jarrell's reputation become of a size to distinguish him from the other important young poets who were prominent and promising in the late forties? Most critics predicted the emerging greatness of a Robert Lowell or a Karl Shapiro, but few guessed that Jarrell would outstrip them, especially in so short a time.

Normally enough, it is the quality of his poetry that has done it. It is possible, though it is an academic question, that the best poems of some of Jarrell's contemporaries equal his best; but none of the poets of his generation has produced so much that is so consistently good. It is more, though, than this quantity of quality. It is more, even, than the originality, dramatic force, and universality of his poetry; or than the suppleness and audibility, which one immediately associates with Jarrell's work. What, then, is that quality that almost any reader senses at once in such poems as 'Eighth Air Force', 'Losses', 'A Girl in a Library', and 'A Game at Salzburg'? It is Protean and difficult to name. Is it an attitude toward man that is wholly compassionate and, yet, pained at his ridiculous shortcomings? That almost religious ambivalence—like Rilke's—like Blake's—that tries passionately to consummate the marriage of Heaven and Hell? Or has Jarrell himself named it (many times) in lines like these:

> I have suffered in a dream, because of him,
> Many things; for this last saviour, man,

> I have lied as I lie now. But what is lying?
> Men wash their hands, in blood, as best they can:
> I find no fault in this just man.

One must turn to the namable, to such things as originality, techniques, and subject matter.

Originality in verse of the last decade or two is, on the whole, weak. Too much brilliant experimentation in the work of Whitman, Hopkins, Pound, and Eliot had preceded it. The greatest danger to the emergent poet of recent years has been his armor of technique—of experimental rhythms and verse forms, of symbolic images, expanded diction, and even of settled subject matter. With Jarrell this armor has been a linked and loosely woven one, rather than a solid sheet. It would be absurd to deny that Jarrell has been influenced by earlier twentieth-century writers, but the influence is submerged or absorbed to such a degree that it is rare that one detects echoes or imitations. His most suspected sires are Yeats in techniques and Rilke (or Frost?) in attitudes, although like most creatures, he resembles his grandparents—at least one of them is Browning; another is Blake—more than he does his direct progenitors. Yeats' rhythms, rhymes, and dramatic forms are seen naturalized in Jarrell's verse. It is never 'free verse', it is usually the natural, counterpointed rhythm of speech (Jarrell is no Pope and no Keats), and it is often monologue or dialogue. Jarrell, like Wordsworth, Hopkins, and Frost, ranks among the angels of poetry—those who write for the ear. Thus, his lines always end so that their existence can be heard, and his rhythms are of the richness of formal verse with speech rhythms superimposed on them. It is no coincidence that he has attempted a grassroots campaign to make literate audiences listen to poetry; his poetry must be listened to.

The greatest suspended appeal in Jarrell's poetry is his subject matter. All subject matter, if it is truth, is universal in its appeal; but the use of subject is not always so widely available as is Jarrell's. He writes mostly of dreams, a child's fairy-tale view, of wars. He frequently combines these in what Sister Bernetta Quinn has called 'the metamorphic tradition', where change is the normal process, as it is in the dream, in the fairy tale, in the child's imagination, and, perversely, in war. It is just here, in the universal will to change focus and shape that much of the appeal of Jarrell's poetry lies. But the poet does more than to arouse this inchoate urge; there is something much more powerful when, with paternal firmness and gentleness, he destroys our dream and our freedom at the moment he has given it to us. In such moments as 'Behind everything there is always The unknown unwanted life' we are forced to eat of the unbearable Tree of Knowledge. It is consistent that the other important mode of Jarrell's writing —found mostly in his fiction and criticism—is satire and invective, the negative literary means of transforming.

Like Rilke, another believer in 'little people', Jarrell has found his common touch within, rather than without. In turning inwards in dreams, or backwards in 'Märchen', or roundabout with the child, he achieves the common touch; although not in a boisterous or extroverted or folksy way of a Kipling, a Browning, or a Carl Sandburg. That a general audience is thus touched and toppled is no sleight of hand. It is, as the poet who wrote 'Children Selecting Books in a Library' and 'La Belle au Bois Dormant' well knows, the unpremeditated, unknown even, response to universal desires and fears. 'Have we not learned', the poet tells us, 'from tales

> Neither of beasts nor kingdoms nor their Lord,
> But of our own hearts, the realm of death—
> Neither to rule nor die? to change, to change!'

Woman's College ROBERT HUMPHREY
University of North Carolina

Randall Jarrell: A Bibliography

I. Books by Randall Jarrell

1. BLOOD FOR A STRANGER, First Edition, 1942.

BLOOD FOR | A STRANGER | by | RANDALL JARRELL | *Muss es sein?* | *Es muss sein!* | *Es muss sein!* | HARCOURT, BRACE AND COMPANY, NEW YORK

Gathered in six signatures: [1-6⁸]; top, fore, and bottom edges trimmed; plain white end papers; binding, 8¾ × 5¾ inches, in bright red cloth with lettering stamped in blue running from the top: Randall Jarrell [dot] Blood for a Stranger [at foot of spine in two lines] Harcourt, Brace | and Company; dust jacket printed in bright red with white lettering on the cover and the spine, and printed in red letters on the white paper on the back and on the flaps.

Collation: One leaf; [i] half title; [ii] blank; [iii] title page; [iv] reads: COPYRIGHT, 1942, BY | HARCOURT, BRACE AND COMPANY, INC. | *All rights reserved, including | the right to reproduce this book | or portions thereof in any form.* | *first edition* | PRINTED IN THE UNITED STATES OF AMERICA; [v] dedication: TO | ALLEN TATE; [vi] blank; [vii] note: Some of these poems have been printed in the | *Southern Review, Kenyon Review, Partisan Re-* | *view, New Republic, Poetry, Transition* [sic], *Ameri-* | *can Review, Atlantic* [*Monthly*, and *New Yorker*; | and in a book, *Five Young American Poets*.; [viii] blank; ix-x, Contents; [1] a large number one; [2] blank; 3-82, text, except [23] with large number two and [24] blank, [42] blank, [43] with large number three and [44] blank, [63] with large number four and [64] blank; one blank leaf.

An edition of 1,700 copies was printed July 6, 1942. In an advertisement in the *Publishers' Weekly* for September 26, 1942 (p. 1111), *Blood for a Stranger* was announced for publication September 24, 1942, for $2.00 and was listed in the Weekly Record in the same issue as published. No other printing was made.

[15]

Contents (in four parts):

1.
On the Railway Platform
London
The Lost Love
90 North
A Story
1938: Tales from the Vienna Woods
A Little Poem
Fat, Aging, the Child clinging to Her Hand . . .
Children Selecting Books in a Library
A Poem for Someone Killed in Spain
For an Emigrant

2.
The Iceberg
Because of Me, Because of You . . .
The Bad Music
The Blind Sheep
1789–1939
The Ways and the Peoples
The Refugees
Love, in Its Separate Being . . .
The Hanged Man on the Gallows . . .
A Picture in the Paper
The Cow Wandering in the Bare Field . . .
When You and I Were All . . .

3.
For the Madrid Road
The Automaton
Over the Florid Capitals . . .
Kirilov on a Skyscraper
Up in the Sky . . .
The Winter's Tale
Jack
Esthetic Theories: Art as Expression
Dummies
An Essay on the Human Will
The See-er of Cities
A Description of Some Confederate Soldiers

4.
The Head of Wisdom
1938: The Spring Dances
Fear
The Machine-Gun
The Memoirs of Glückel of Hameln
Song: Not There
The Long Vacation
The Skaters
The Christmas Roses
Variations
Che Faro Senza Euridice

Three of these poems, 1938: Tales from the Vienna Woods; Jack; and Memoirs of Glückel of Hameln, were first published in this volume. All the other poems were published previously in the periodicals noted above in the collation for p. [vii].

2. LITTLE FRIEND, LITTLE FRIEND, First Edition, 1945.

LITTLE FRIEND, | *LITTLE FRIEND* | By RANDALL JAR-RELL | [line of diamond-shaped ornaments in blue] | . . . . *Then I heard the bomber call me in:* | [rule in blue] | *"Little Friend, Little Friend, I got two* | [rule in blue] | *engines on fire. Can you see me, Little* | [rule in blue] | *Friend?"* | [rule in blue] | *I said "I'm crossing right over you.* | [rule in blue] | *Let's go home."* | [line of diamond-shaped ornaments in blue] | DIAL PRESS [dot] 1945 [dot] NEW YORK

Gathered in four signatures: [1–4⁸]; top, fore, and bottom edges trimmed; top edge stained blue; binding, 9½ × 6⅛ inches, in deep blue cloth with small dark stars stamped irregularly on the front cover in blind and a press mark stamped in the lower right hand corner on the back cover in blind; spine stamped in yellow with blue showing through as ornament and reading from the top down: JARRELL [break in design] LITTLE FRIEND, LITTLE FRIEND [break in design] DIAL; dust jacket: front and spine in brown and black, with lettering in white and black, the back cover and flaps of jacket printed in black.

Collation: One leaf blank; [1] half title; [2] blank; [3] title page; [4] reads: Copyright, 1945, by Dial Press | Designed by Meyer Wagman | *Some of these poems have been published* | *in Partisan Review, The Nation, The New* | *Republic, The Kenyon Review, and Poetry.* | *This book is complete and unabridged in con-* | *tents, and is manufactured in strict conformity* | *with Government regulations for saving paper.* | Printed in the United States of America | by the Haddon Craftsmen, Inc. Scranton, Pa.; [5] dedication: TO | SARA STARR; [6] blank; [7-8] Contents; [9] second half title; [10] blank; 11-58, text; two leaves blank.

An edition of 2,000 copies was printed October 23, 1945, according to the publisher, and was listed in the *Publishers' Weekly*, October 27, 1945, in the Weekly Record as published for $2.00.

Contents:

2nd Air Force
A Pilot from the Carrier
The Emancipators
Losses
The Dream of Waking
Leave
Siegfried
Mother, Said the Child
The Carnegie Library, Juvenile Division
Soldier (T. P.)
A Front
The Learners
Gunner
Port of Embarkation
Come to the Stone
The Metamorphoses
Absent with Official Leave
Mail Call

The Angels at Hamburg
Protocols
The Snow-Leopard
The Boyg, Peer Gynt, the One Only One
The Difficult Resolution
1914
The Soldier Walks Under the Trees of the University
A Lullaby
The Soldier
The Sick Nought
Prisoners
An Officers' Prison Camp Seen from a Troop Train
The State
The Wide Prospect
The Death of the Ball Turret Gunner

Two of these poems: The Snow-Leopard and The State, were first published in the *Sewanee Review*. All of the others were previously published in the periodicals listed on page [4] of this volume as noted above in the collation.

3. LOSSES, First Edition, 1948.

LOSSES | RANDALL JARRELL | NEW YORK | HARCOURT, BRACE AND COMPANY

Gathered in five signatures: [1-5⁸]; top, fore, and bottom edges trimmed; plain white end papers; binding, 8¼ × 5½ inches, in smooth black cloth with lettering in gold on the spine running from the top: LOSSES [space] Randall Jarrell [space] HARCOURT, BRACE | AND COMPANY; dust jacket: front and spine printed in gray with lettering LOSSES [in white] | [ornament in red] | POEMS BY | RANDALL | JARRELL [in black] | [all surrounded by red ornamental frame]; back cover and flaps printed in black with a portrait of the author on the back.

Collation: [i] half title; [ii] lists books by the same author; [iii] title page; [iv] reads: COPYRIGHT, 1948, BY | HARCOURT, BRACE AND COMPANY, INC. | *All rights reserved including | the right to reproduce this book | or portions thereof in any form.* | first edition | PRINTED IN THE UNITED STATES OF AMERICA; [v] dedication: To | TOM MERCER; [vi] blank; [vii] note: Most of these poems have already been printed in | *The Nation, Partisan Review, The Kenyon Review, The Sewanee Review, The Virginia Quarterly Re- | view, The Quarterly Review of Literature,* and | *Horizon.*; [viii] blank; [ix] Contents; [x] blank; [1] second half title; [2] blank; 3–63, text; [64] blank; 65–68, Notes; one blank leaf.

An edition of 1,000 copies printed, according to the records in the publisher's office, on February 24, 1948. It was announced in the Spring Book List, 1948, of the *Publishers' Weekly* for publication on March 4 at $2.00, and listed in the April 3, 1948 issue (153:1595) as published.

Contents:

Lady Bates
The Dead Wingman
A Camp in the Prussian Forest
Money
Pilots, Man Your Planes
Stalag Luft
The Place of Death
O My Name It Is Sam Hall
Eighth Air Force
The Lines
The Dead in Melanesia
The Rising Sun
A Country Life
Burning the Letters
The Breath of Night
Sears Roebuck
Jews at Haifa

A Field Hospital
When I Was Home Last Christmas
New Georgia
The Range in the Desert
In the Camp There Was One Alive
A Ward in the States
The Märchen
The Child of Courts
The Subway from New Britain to the Bronx
1945: The Death of the Gods
Moving
Loss
In the Ward: the Sacred Wood
Orestes at Tauris
Notes

A note inside the front flap of the jacket says this 'third volume of verse ... contains thirty new poems and a long narrative poem from an earlier period'. Three of these poems first appeared in this volume: A Country Life; When I Was Home Last Christmas; and Moving. All the other poems had appeared previously in the periodicals listed on page [vii] and noted in the collation above.

3a. LOSSES, Reissue, 1954.

LOSSES | RANDALL JARRELL | NEW YORK | HARCOURT, BRACE AND COMPANY

The format and binding of this reissue are the same as the first edition, 1948; the dust jacket has been redesigned with the front and spine in black with white and green swirls around areas with the title, etc.; the dust jacket advertises Jarrell's *The Seven-League Crutches*, 1951.

Changes in collation from the first edition, 1948, for the 1954 reissue are: [ii] added title, *The Seven-League Crutches*; [iv] omits the words, 'first edition'.

A reissue of 1,000 copies, according to the records in the publisher's office, was made in January 1954. It was advertised in the Spring Book Index, 1954, of the *Publishers' Weekly* for publication on March 4, 1954 and listed in the April 10 issue as published by Harcourt for $3.00 with the note: 'Has been out-of-print. Formerly published at $2.'

4. THE SEVEN-LEAGUE CRUTCHES, First Edition, 1951.

RANDALL JARRELL | [swelled rule] | *The* | SEVEN - LEAGUE | CRUTCHES | [swelled rule] | NEW YORK | HARCOURT, BRACE AND COMPANY

Gathered in six signatures: [1–6^8]; top, fore, and bottom edges trimmed; plain white end papers; binding, 8¼ × 5½ inches, in plain black cloth with gold lettering on the spine reading from the top: THE SEVEN-LEAGUE CRUTCHES [space] Randall Jarrell [space] HARCOURT, BRACE | AND COMPANY; dust jacket: bright yellow paper printed in terra cotta and black on the front and spine with lettering in yellow on the front, printed in black and terra cotta on back and on the flaps.

Collation: [1] half title; [2] lists the four books by Randall Jarrell including this one; [3] title page; [4] reads: COPYRIGHT, 1951, BY RANDALL JARRELL | *All rights reserved, including the right* | *to reproduce this book or portions thereof in any form.* | *first edition* | To | MACKIE | These poems have already been printed in *Poetry*, *The Kenyon* | *Review*, *The Nation*, *Botteghe Oscure*, *The Virginia Quarterly Re-* | *view*, *Partisan Review*, and *The Sewanee Review*. I'd like to thank | these magazines for permission to reprint the poems; and to thank | the John Simon Guggenheim Memorial Foundation for the oppor- | tunity to write several of them. | PRINTED IN THE UNITED STATES OF AMERICA; [5–6] Contents; 7–94, text, except pages [48] and [70] which are unnumbered and blank; one blank leaf.

An edition of 2,000 copies was printed on August 15, 1951, according to the publisher's records. It was announced in the Fall Book Index, 1951, of the *Publishers' Weekly* for publication on October 4 and was listed in the issue for October 6 (160:1542) as published at $2.75.

A set of 'Advance Uncorrected Proofs' (twenty-five sheets) is in the WCUNC Library. These sheets were sent out by the publisher for review with a covering advance notice.

Contents (in three sections):

Europe
The Orient Express
A Game at Salzburg
A Soul
Hohensalzburg: Fantastic Variations on a Theme of Romantic Character
An English Garden in Austria
The Face
The Knight, Death, and the Devil
Nollekens
The Truth
The Contrary Poet
A Rhapsody on Irish Themes
The Olive Garden
A Conversation with the Devil
Children
A Sick Child
The Black Swan

A Quilt-Pattern
Afterwards
The Night Before the Night Before Christmas
Once Upon a Time
A Girl in a Library
The Sleeping Beauty: Variation of the Prince
La Belle au Bois Dormant
The Island
Hope
Good-Bye, Wendover; Good-Bye, Mountain Home
Transient Barracks
Terms
Jonah
The Venetian Blind
Seele Im Raum

The poem, A Rhapsody on Irish Themes, was first published in this volume. All the other poems were first published in the magazines listed on page [4] and noted in the collation above. The notice on the inside front flap of the jacket states there are twenty-eight poems in this book, while actually there are twenty-nine.

5. POETRY AND THE AGE, First Edition, 1953.

Randall Jarrell | [rule] | POETRY | AND | THE AGE | [publisher's device] | [rule] | Alfred A. Knopf: New York | 1953

Gathered in ten signatures: [1–5^{16}, 6^8, 7^{16}, 8^8, 9–10^{16}]; top edge trimmed and stained light green, fore and bottom edge rough trimmed; binding, 8⅝ × 5¾ inches, in black cloth with author's name stamped in blind between rules on front cover, and stamped in gold on the spine: Randall | Jarrell | [ornamental rule] | POETRY | AND | THE AGE | [ornamental rule] | Alfred A. | Knopf; plain white end papers; dust jacket printed in two strips of green with lettering in white, red, and green; statements printed in green and red on the back and on the flaps.

Collation: One blank leaf; one leaf with recto blank and verso with books by Randall Jarrell; [i] half title; [ii] blank; [iii] title page; [iv] [twenty-two lines in italic type of permissions] | L. C. catalog card number: 52-12173 | [next two lines boxed by a thick and thin rule with side ornaments] THIS IS A BORZOI BOOK | PUBLISHED BY ALFRED [dot] A [dot] KNOPF, INC. | *Copyright 1953 by* RANDALL JARRELL. [The

A BIBLIOGRAPHY 21

remainder of line and five additional lines in italic type restricting permission to reprint and note that it is published simultaneously in Canada by McClelland & Stewart Limited.₁ | FIRST EDITION; ₍v₎ dedication: TO | Mary von Schrader; ₍vi₎ blank; vii, Preface; ₍viii₎ blank; ix-x, Contents; ₍1₎ second half title; ₍2₎ blank; 3-271, text; ₍272₎ A NOTE ON THE TYPE | ₍fourteen lines in italic type₎ | *The book was composed, printed and bound by* | KINGSPORT PRESS, INC., *Kingsport, Tennessee.* | *Designed by* HARRY FORD; one blank leaf.

An edition of 2,000 copies was printed, August 1953, and the following month, September 1953, a second printing of 1,750 copies was made. It was listed in the Summer Book Index, 1953, in the *Publishers' Weekly* for publication August 17, 1953, and announced as published in the August 22 issue at $4.00. Copies of the second printing state on verso of title page: 'Published August 17, 1953. Second Printing, October 1953'.

Contents:

The Obscurity of the Poet
Two Essays on Robert Frost
   The Other Frost
   To the Laodiceans
The Age of Criticism
John Ransom's Poetry
Some Lines from Whitman
Reflections on Wallace Stevens
A Verse Chronicle
  I *Walter de la Mare*
  II *Alex Comfort*
  III *Tristan Corbière*
  IV *Muriel Rukeyser*

v *R. P. Blackmur*
VI *Anthologies*
VII *Bad Poets*
Two Essays on Marianne Moore
   The Humble Animal
   Her Shield
From the Kingdom of Necessity
Poets
An Introduction to the *Selected Poems of*
   William Carlos Williams
Three Books
The Situation of a Poet

'All of these pieces—with the exception of the introduction to William Carlos Williams' *Selected Poems*—have been published in magazines, some of them in different shape. I want to thank *Partisan Review*, *The Nation*, *The Kenyon Review*, *The New York Times Book Review*, and *Perspectives U. S. A.* both for printing them and for allowing me to reprint them. . . .', from the Preface, page vii.

5a. POETRY AND THE AGE, Vintage Books, 1955.

Randall Jarrell | ₍ornamental rule₎ | POETRY | AND | THE AGE | ₍ornamental rule₎ | New York: Vintage Books | 1955

A paper-bound edition (Vintage Books, K12), 7¼ × 4⅜ inches; front, spine, and back in black, yellow, gray, and red with the words POETRY and THE AGE in ornamental capitals in white outlined in black on the front cover; all edges trimmed flush with the covers; cover designed by Harry Ford.

Collation: ₍i₎ half title; ₍ii₎ blank; ₍iii₎ title page; ₍iv₎ reads: ₍twenty-two lines of permissions in italic type₎ | Published by Vintage Books, Inc. | Reprinted by arrangement with Alfred A. Knopf, Inc. | First Edition 1953. Reprinted once. | [copyright notice in seven lines of italic type] | FIRST VINTAGE EDITION; [v] dedication; [vi] Preface; [vii–viii] Contents; [1] second half title; [2] blank; [3]–246, text, but with no numbering on pages beginning each article; one leaf: recto, with note on Randall Jarrell, the type in which the book is set and notes on printing; verso, list of Vintage Books, through K14.

An edition of 17,550 was printed January 1955 and a second printing of 7,500 made in November 1955. It was announced as published in the January 29, 1955 issue of the *Publishers' Weekly*.

Contents are the same as in the first edition, 1953.

5b. POETRY AND THE AGE, English Edition, 1955.

RANDALL JARRELL | *Poetry and the Age* | FABER AND FABER LIMITED | 24 Russell Square | London

Gathered in fifteen signatures: [A^8], B–P^8; top, fore, and bottom edges trimmed; white end papers; binding, 8¾ × 5⅞ inches, in plain red cloth with lettering in gold on the spine: Poetry & | the Age | Randall | Jarrell | Faber; dust jacket yellow with design in gray and all the lettering in black; flap inside back cover has quotations from reviews for his *Pictures from an Institution* from English journals.

Collation: [1–2] blank; [3] half title; [4] has the English books 'by the same author'; [5] title page; [6] *First published in mcmlv | by Faber and Faber Limited* | [four additional lines in italic type]; [7] dedication; [8] blank; 9–10, Contents; 11, Acknowledgements; [12] blank; 13, Preface; [14] blank; 15–240, text.

An edition of 2,000 copies was published April 7, 1955. Contents are the same as in the American first edition, 1953.

5c. POETRY AND THE AGE, Italian Edition, 1956.

RANDALL JARRELL | LA POESIA | DI UN'EPOCA | Traduzione e note | di | DONATELLA MANGANOTTI | GUANDA | 1956

Gathered in sixteen signatures: [a]^4, 1–15^8; stiff white paper covers, 9¼ × 6 inches; top uncut, and front and bottom edges rough trimmed; front cover and spine printed in black and green; dust jacket with a photographic view of New York City through the Brooklyn Bridge and blue, red, and yellow colors imposed on the photograph.

Collation: one leaf blank; [iii] series note: NUOVA | COLLANA DI CULTURA | 2; [iv] blank; [v] title page; [vi] reads: Titolo originale dell'opera: POETRY AND THE AGE | Edito da: ALFRED A. KNOPF, Inc. | 501 Madison Avenue—NEW YORK CITY | PROPRIETÀ LETTERARIA | [rule] | Ugo Guanda Editore: Via Contelli,

13—Parma 1956; [vii] PREFAZIONE DELL'AUTORE; [viii] blank; [1]–234, text, with numbering for pages beginning new chapters omitted and [180] and [192] blank; [235] INDICE; [236] blank; [237] table of contents; [238] blank; [239] reads: FINITO DI STAMPARE | PER ORDINE E CONTO DI UGO GUANDA EDITORE | IL 20 NOVEMBRE 1956 | DALLA S. P. A. POLIGRAFICI IL RESTO DEL CARLINO | DI BOLOGNA; [240] blank.

Notes identifying and explaining references in the essays are placed at the foot of many of the pages throughout the text.

Contents in translation and arrangement of the chapters in this volume are the same as in the first edition of *Poetry and the Age*.

6. PICTURES FROM AN INSTITUTION, First Edition, 1954.

A Comedy by | *Randall Jarrell* | NEW YORK [small space] ALFRED A. KNOPF [small space] 1954 | [all on one page. On facing page:] *Pictures* | FROM AN | *Institution* | [publisher's device]

Gathered in ten signatures: [1–2^{16}, 3^8, 4–7^{16}, 8^8, 9–10^{16}]; top edge trimmed and stained a reddish brown, fore and bottom edges rough trimmed; binding, 8⅜ × 5⅝ inches, in a blue cloth, stamped in blind on the cover: [rule] | Randall Jarrell | [rule], and the publisher's device on the back in blind; the spine stamped in gold reads: *Randall* | *Jarrell* | *Pictures* FROM AN *Institution* [running vertically] | *Alfred A.* | *Knopf*; plain white end papers; dust jacket printed in green, black, and reddish brown, with a portrait of the author on inside rear flap and note on inside front flap reads: *Jacket design:* HARRY FORD.

Collation: One leaf: recto blank and verso with books by the author; [i] half title; [ii–iii] title pages; [iv] PICTURES FROM AN INSTITUTION *is a work of fiction. The details, the | names, the characters, and the Institution are not intended to, and | do not, relate to any existing institution or to any real person | living or dead.* | L. C. catalog card number: 54–5973 | THIS IS A BORZOI BOOK | PUBLISHED BY ALFRED A. KNOPF, INC. | *Copyright 1952, 1953, 1954* by RANDALL JARRELL. [Seven lines in italic type] | FIRST EDITION; [v] dedication: TO *Mary* AND *Hannah*; [vi] blank; vii, Contents; [viii] blank; [1] title of chapter one; [2] blank; 3–277, text, except for blank pages and chapter heading pages unnumbered [32–34, 76–78, 129–130, 184–186, 233–234, 249–250]; [278] A NOTE ON THE TYPE | [fourteen lines in italic type] | [publisher's device] | *Composed, printed, and bound by* KINGSPORT PRESS, | INC., *Kingsport, Tennessee.* | *Designed by* HARRY FORD.

An edition of 6,000 copies was printed in May 1954; a second printing of 1,500 in June 1954; a third printing of 1,500 copies in August 1954; and a fourth printing of 2,000 copies in January 1955. Indications of later printings are indicated on page [vi] in the place of note for the first edition. This note on a later printing indicates first printing as May 3, 1954. It was announced in the *Publishers' Weekly*, May 8, 1954, as published for $3.50.

Contents (some of these chapters were first printed as separate stories and are indexed in Part IV, Prose, of this bibliography):

1 The President, Mrs., and Derek Robbins
2 The Whittakers and Gertrude*
3 Miss Batterson and Benton
4 Constance and the Rosenbaums*
5 Gertrude and Sidney
6 Art Night
7 They All Go

6a. PICTURES FROM AN INSTITUTION, English Edition, 1954.

PICTURES | FROM AN INSTITUTION | [ornamental line] | A COMEDY BY | RANDALL JARRELL | FABER AND FABER LIMITED | 24 Russell Square | London

Gathered in eighteen signatures: [A⁸], B–R⁸, S+ S*⁸⁺²; top, fore, and bottom edges trimmed; binding, 7½ × 5¼ inches, in green woven cloth with white lettering on spine: Pictures | from an | Institution | BY | Randall | Jarrell | Faber; plain white end papers; dust jacket printed in red and green on front and spine with lettering in black, except for author's name on the spine in red, a picture of the author on the back flap; on front of jacket and on the inside flap: 'Recommended by the Book Society'; the price on the jacket, 12s 6d net; a note on the front flap states, '*Pictures from an Institution* is his first novel and his first book to be published in this country'.

Collation: [1–2] blank; [3] half title; [4] blank; [5] title page; [6] reads: *First published in Great Britain in mcmliv* . . . ; [7] dedication; [8] blank; 9, Contents; [10] blank; 11–290, text; one blank leaf.

An edition of 4,944 copies was published October 1, 1954.

Contents: Chapters the same as in the first American edition, 1954.

7. SELECTED POEMS, First Edition, 1955.

SELECTED | POEMS | [rule] | RANDALL | JARRELL | NEW YORK [small space] ALFRED A KNOPF [small space] 1955 | [publisher's mark]

Gathered in eight signatures: [1–2¹⁶, 3⁸, 4–5¹⁶, 6¹², 7–8¹⁶]; top edge trimmed and stained yellow, fore and bottom edges irregularly trimmed; plain white end papers; binding, 8⅝ × 5⅞ inches, in smooth blue cloth; front cover stamped in blind: SELECTED | POEMS | [rule] | RANDALL | JARRELL; spine stamped in gold running from the top: SELECTED POEMS | [gold rule, a strip of gold with lettering showing through in blue, reading horizontally] Alfred A | Knopf [gold rule] RANDALL JARRELL; back cover stamped with publisher's device on lower right hand corner in blind; dust jacket: printed on front and spine solid black with lettering in yellow except for ornamental POEMS in white and yellow on the front, a portrait of the author is on the back. Jacket and the book were designed by Harry Ford. The volume was selected for the A.I.G.A. Fifty Books of the Year, 1955.

A BIBLIOGRAPHY 25

Collation: One leaf: recto blank and verso with books by author; ₍i₎ half title; ₍ii₎ blank; ₍iii₎ title page; ₍iv₎ reads: L. C. catalog card number: 55-5613 | © Randall Jarrell, 1955 | ₍rule₎ | THIS IS A BORZOI BOOK, | PUBLISHED BY ALFRED A. KNOPF, INC. | ₍rule₎ | ₍eight lines in italic type with copyright notices₎ | FIRST EDITION | ₍five lines in italic type with permissions to reprint₎; ₍v₎ dedication: TO | *Mary,* | *Alleyne,* | AND | *Beatrice*; ₍vi₎ blank; vii–xvii, Introduction; ₍xviii₎ blank; xix–xxii, Contents; ₍1₎ reads: SELECTED | POEMS | ₍rule₎ | I ₍roman numeral₎; ₍2₎ blank; 3–132, text for Part I, with pages ₍82₎ and ₍120₎ blank; ₍133₎ reads: SELECTED | POEMS | ₍rule₎ | II ₍roman numeral₎; ₍134₎ blank; 135–205, text for Part II, with page ₍154₎ blank; ₍206₎ reads: A NOTE ON THE TYPE | ₍twenty lines in italic type₎ | *Composed, printed, and bound by* KINGSPORT PRESS, | INC., *Kingsport Tennessee. Paper manufactured by* S. D. | WARREN COMPANY, *Boston, Massachusetts* | *Designed by* HARRY FORD.; one blank leaf.

An edition of 2,000 copies was printed in March 1955. It was announced in the Spring Book Index, 1955, of the *Publishers' Weekly* for publication March 14, and listed as published in the March 19 issue of the *Publishers' Weekly* (167:1601) by Knopf at $4.00. In the copyright notice on page ₍iv₎ it states, 'Published simultaneously in Canada by McClelland & Stewart, Limited'. The publisher writes that 'the Canadian editions are simply bound books that we have supplied our Canadian outlet; these are our original editions with our imprint.'

The 'Author 1st Proof', December 22, 1954, proof sheets dated January 4, 1955, and a set of 'Confirmation Plate Proofs' dated January 17 with full proposed collation are in the Woman's College Library. These contain many manuscript notes and instructions for the printing of the *Selected Poems.*

Contents (in two parts and in thirteen sections):

Introduction
₍Part₎ I
LIVES
   A Girl in a Library
   A Country Life
   The Knight, Death, and the Devil
   The Face
   Lady Bates
   When I Was Home Last Christmas . . .
   A Conversation with the Devil
   Nollekens
   Seele im Raum
   The Night before the Night before Christmas

DREAM-WORK
   A Sick Child
   The Black Swan
   The Venetian Blind
   A Quilt-Pattern
   The Island
   In the Ward: the Sacred Wood

THE WIDE PROSPECT
   The Orient Express
   A Game at Salzburg
   An English Garden in Austria
   A Soul
   A Rhapsody on Irish Themes
   The Memoirs of Glückel of Hameln
   To the New World
   The Märchen
   Hohensalzburg: Fantastic Variations on a Theme of Romantic Character

ONCE UPON A TIME
   Moving
   The Sleeping Beauty: Variations of the Prince
   The Prince
   The Carnegie Library, Juvenile Division
   The Blind Sheep
   The Skaters
   Jonah
   Song: Not There
   Children Selecting Books in a Library

THE WORLD IS EVERYTHING THAT
IS THE CASE
  Sears Roebuck
  A Utopian Journey
  Hope
  90 North
  The Snow-Leopard
  The Boyg, Peer Gynt, the One Only One
  Money
  The Emancipators

[Part] II
BOMBERS
  Eighth Air Force
  The Death of the Ball Turret Gunner
  Losses
  Transient Barracks
  Siegfried

THE CARRIERS
  A Pilot from the Carrier
  Pilots, Man Your Planes
  The Dead Wingman
  Burning the Letters

PRISONERS
  Stalag Luft
  Jews at Haifa
  Prisoners
  O My Name It Is Sam Hall
  A Camp in the Prussian Forest

CAMPS AND FIELDS
  A Lullaby
  Mail Call
  Absent with Official Leave
  A Front
  The Sick Nought
  Leave
  The Range in the Desert
  Second Air Force

  Variations
  Le Poète Contumace

THE GRAVES IN THE FOREST
  La Belle au Bois Dormant
  A Story
  Loss
  The Breath of Night
  Afterwards
  The Place of Death

THE TRADES
  The Rising Sun
  New Georgia
  The Subway from New Britain to the
    Bronx
  1945: The Death of the Gods
  A Ward in the States
  The Wide Prospect
  The Dead in Melanesia

CHILDREN AND CIVILIANS
  The State
  Come to the Stone . . .
  The Angels at Hamburg
  Protocols
  The Metamorphoses
  The Truth

SOLDIERS
  Port of Embarkation
  The Lines
  A Field Hospital
  1914
  Gunner
  Good-bye, Wendover; Good-bye,
    Mountain Home
  The Survivor among Graves
  A War
  Terms

On the back jacket flap it states: 'There are 104 poems in all [actually there are only 94], a number of them revised for this occasion . . .' Randall Jarrell wrote in the *Introduction*, page vii, 'in this *Selected Poems* there are ten poems from my first book, some of them a great deal changed; almost all the other poems come from *Losses*, *The Seven-League Crutches*, or *Little Friend, Little Friend*. . . . Only two poems, "A War" and "The Survivor Among Graves", are new.'

7a. SELECTED POEMS, English Edition, 1956.
SELECTED POEMS | [star] | RANDALL JARRELL | FABER AND FABER LIMITED | 24 Russell Square | London

Gathered in fourteen signatures: [A^8], B-O^8; all edges trimmed; binding, 8¼ × 5½ inches, in mulberry-colored cloth with lettering on the spine in gold: Selected | Poems | [star] | Randall | Jarrell | Faber; plain white end papers; dust jacket in light gray printed in black with three bands of vertical ornamental rules in blue on front cover and spine; on back and inside rear flap of jacket are quotations from reviews of his *Pictures from an Institution* and *Poetry and the Age* which had appeared in English journals.

Collation: [1] half title; [2] *by the same author* | [star] | PICTURES FROM AN INSTITUTION | POETRY AND THE AGE; [3] title page; [4] *This selection first published in mcmlvi | by Faber and Faber Limited | 24 Russell Square London W.C.1 | Printed in Great Britain | at the Bowering Press Plymouth | All rights reserved;* [5] dedication as in first American edition, 1955; [6] blank; 7-10, Contents; 11, Acknowledgements; [12] blank; 13-23, Introduction; [24] blank; [25] Part One; [26] blank; 27-154, text same as in the first American edition, 1955, with section headings; [155] Part Two; [156] blank; 157 223, text same as in the first American edition, 1955, with section headings; [224] blank.

An edition of 1,735 copies was published on January 27, 1956.

Contents: The same as in the first American edition, 1955. There were a few changes noted: the order of a paragraph in the Introduction of the English edition was reversed and a note as in the original printing in the periodical was added to the poem Pilots, Man Your Planes on page 167.

II. Collections Indexed for Contributions by Randall Jarrell: Arranged by Title of Collection

American Anthology, ed. by Tom Boggs. Prairie City, Ill.: Press of James A. Decker, 1942.
pp. 49–50: The Head of Wisdom.
American Sampler, a Selection of New Poetry, ed. by Francis Coleman Rosenberger. Iowa City: The Prairie Press, 1951.
pp. 49–50: The Place of Death.
The American Treasury, 1455–1955, ed. by Clifton Fadiman. N. Y.: Harper, 1955.
p. 617: The Death of the Ball Turret Gunner.
American Writers Today, by Alexander Cowie. Stockholm: Radiotjänst, 1956.
pp. 198–204: reprint of selection from 'The Age of Criticism', entitled here 'Poetry and the Age'.
Anthologie de la Poésie Américaine, ed. by Alain Bosquet. Paris: Librairie Stock, 1956.
pp. 240–241: Losses, and its translations, Pertes; pp. 241–242: The Sick Nought, and its translation, Le Zero Malade.
Antología de la Poesía Norteamericana Contemporánea, selección, traducción y estudio preliminar de Eugenio Florit. Washington, D. C.: Pan American Union, 1955.
pp. 132–134: The Survivor Among Graves, and its translation, El Vivo entre las Tumbas.
An Approach to Literature, by Cleanth Brooks, John Thibaut Purser, and Robert Penn Warren. N. Y.: Appleton-Century-Crofts, 1952. 3rd edition.
pp. 365–367: Burning the Letters (followed by an 'Exercise' on the poem); pp. 397–399: Eighth Air Force (followed by an analysis).
The Best American Short Stories, 1954, ed. by Martha Foley. Boston: Houghton, Mifflin, 1954.
pp. 185–205: Gertrude and Sidney; (p. 412: Biographical note on Randall Jarrell).
Best Articles, 1953, selected by Rudolf Flesch. N. Y.: Hermitage House, 1953.
pp. 203–222: The Age of Criticism.

Borestone Mountain Poetry Awards. Philadelphia: University of Pennsylvania Press.
   1952, p. 4: The Black Swan.
   1953, pp. 43-44: The Survivor Among Graves.
The Criterion Book of Modern American Verse, ed. with introduction by Wystan H. Auden. New York: Criterion Books, 1956. (Also published in London as *Faber Book of Modern American Verse* by Faber and Faber, 1956).
   pp. 276-278: The Lines; The Breath of Night; The Knight, Death and the Devil.
Essays Today, 2, ed. by Richard M. Ludwig. New York: Harcourt, Brace and Company, 1956.
   pp. 129-134: The Intellectual in America.
Fifteen Modern American Poets, ed. by George P. Elliott. New York: Rinehart, 1956. (Rinehart Edition, 79)
   pp. 42-61: A Girl in the Library; Seele im Raum; The Black Swan; The Orient Express; The Märchen; The Sleeping Beauty: Variation of the Prince; A Utopian Journey; 90 North; Loss; The Death of the Ball Turret Gunner; Losses; A Lullaby; 2nd Air Force; A Ward in the States; The Metamorphoses.
Five Young American Poets. Norfolk, Conn.: New Directions, 1940.
   pp. 81-123: 'The Rage for the Lost Penny' (title for collection of poems), portrait; p. 84: For the Madrid Road, in facsimile of handwriting; pp. 85-90: A Note on Poetry; pp. 91-123: On the Railway Platform; The Ways and the Peoples; Love, in its Separate Being . . .; The See-er of Cities; When You and I were All . . .; A Description of Some Confederate Soldiers; The Automaton; The Winter's Tale; A Poem for Someone Killed in Spain; The Refugees; A Story; The Machine-Gun; Eine Kleine Nachtmusik; 1789-1939; Because of Me, Because of You . . .; The Bad Music; A Little Poem; For the Madrid Road; Che Faro Senza Euridice; For an Emigrant.
Golden Horizon, ed. by Cyril Connolly. London: Weidenfeld & Nicolson, 1953.
   p. 100: The Death of the Ball Turret Gunner.
Invitation to Poetry, a Round of Poems from John Skelton to Dylan Thomas, arranged with comments by Lloyd Frankenberg. New York: Doubleday & Company, 1956.
   pp. 251-252: A Sick Child.

Kenyon Critics, Studies in Modern Literature from the Kenyon Review, ed. by John Crowe Ransom. Cleveland: World Publishing Co., 1951.

pp. 277–280: The Humble Animal.

Literature in America, an Anthology of Literary Criticism, selected and introduced by Philip Rahv. New York: Meridian Books, 1945.

pp. 342–349: Introduction to W. C. Williams.

The Literature of the South, ed. by Richmond C. Beatty and others. Chicago: Scott, Foresman, 1952.

(p. 811: Randall Jarrell, 1914–); pp. 811–815: The Head of Wisdom; For an Emigrant.

Literary Opinion in America, ed. by Morton Dauwen Zabel, revised ed. New York: Harper, 1951.

pp. 742–748: The End of the Line (revised version reprinted from the *Nation*, 154:222–228, Feb. 21, 1942).

Mid-Century American Poets, ed. by John Ciardi. New York: Twayne, 1950.

pp. 158–167: Robert Lowell's Poetry; pp. 182–201: Answer to Questions (12 comments on poetry); The State; A Camp in the Prussian Forest; Port of Embarkation; The Dead Wingman; Eighth Air Force; Siegfried; A Game at Salzburg; Variations; Burning the Letters; The Dead in Melanesia; A Country Life; The Death of the Ball Turret Gunner; Lady Bates.

Modern American Poetry . . . combined mid-century edition, ed. by Louis Untermeyer. New York: Harcourt, Brace & Co., 1950.

pp. 678–686: A Camp in the Prussian Forest; Pilots, Man Your Planes; The Death of the Ball Turret Gunner; Burning the Letters; Jews at Haifa; A Country Life; Hope; The Refugees.

Modern American & Modern British Poetry, ed. by Louis Untermeyer in consultation with Karl Shapiro and Richard Wilbur. New York: Harcourt, Brace & Co., 1955. Rev., shorter ed.

pp. 375–380: Burning the Letters; Hope; The Refugees; 90 North; Pilots, Man Your Planes.

Modern Poetry, American and British, ed. by Kimon Friar and John Malcolm Brinnin. New York: Appleton-Century-Crofts, Inc., 1951.

pp. 384–386: The Snow-Leopard; A Pilot from the Carrier; 90 North.

The New Partisan Reader, 1945–1953, ed. by William Phillips and Philip Rahv. New York: Harcourt, Brace and Co., 1953.
  pp. 164–166: Jews at Haifa; The Death of the Ball Turret Gunner; pp. 408–421: Reflections on Wallace Stevens and E. E. Cummings.
New Poems, 1942. An Anthology of British and American Verse, ed. by Oscar Williams. Mount Vernon, N. Y.: Peter Pauper Press, 1942.
  pp. 116–121: A Poem (same as 'A Picture in the Paper'); 90 North; The Long Vacation; The Difficult Resolution; (at end of volume: a picture of Randall Jarrell in badminton tournament).
New Poems, An Anthology of British and American Verse, ed. by Oscar Williams. New York: Howell, Soskin.
  1943, pp. 109–121: Pictures from a World: Orestes at Tauris; (p. 316: portrait and biographical note).
  1944, pp. 237–238: The Soldier Walks Under the Trees of the University.
A New Southern Harvest, and Anthology, ed. by Robert Penn Warren and Albert Erskine. New York: Bantam Books, 1957.
  pp. 147–164: Gertrude and Sidney.
North Carolina Poetry, ed. by Richard Walser. Richmond: Garrett & Massie, 1951. Rev. ed.
  (pp. 163–167: Randall Jarrell's biographical sketch); pp. 164–167: Lady Bates; A Country Life.
Oxford Book of American Verse . . ., chosen by Francis Otto Matthiessen. New York: Oxford, 1950.
  pp. 1084–1092: For an Emigrant; The Soldier Walks Under the Trees of the University; The Sick Nought; Prisoners; The Death of the Ball Turret Gunner; Losses.
The Partisan Reader, Ten Years of the Partisan Review, 1934–44: An Anthology. New York: Dial, 1946.
  pp. 239–240: A Nursery Rhyme; p. 283: The Metamorphoses; pp. 629–633: Poetry in a Dry Season.
Penguin Book of Modern American Verse, selected by Geoffrey Moore. London: Penguin Books, 1954.
  (pp. 268–269: Randall Jarrell, critical comments); pp. 269–274: The Death of the Ball Turret Gunner; The Knight, Death and the Devil; A Girl in the Library.
Poetry Awards, see *Borestone Mountain Poetry Awards*
Reading Modern Poetry, ed. by Paul Engle and Warren Carrier. Chi-

cago: Scott, Foresman, 1955.

    pp. 223–236: Eighth Air Force; Siegfried.

Readings for Liberal Education, ed. by Louis G. Locke, William M. Gibson, and George Arms, rev. ed. New York: Rinehart, 1954. Part II, Introduction to Literature.

    pp. 279–280: On Lowell's Where the Rainbow Ends.

The Sound of Wings, Readings for the Air Age, ed. by Joseph B. Roberts and Paul L. Briand. New York: Henry Holt, 1957.

    p. 201: The Death of the Ball Turret Gunner; pp. 206–207: 2nd Air Force; pp. 218–220: Siegfried.

A Southern Vanguard, ed. by Allen Tate. New York: Prentice-Hall, 1947.

    pp. 153–155: The Märchen.

Spearhead, 10 Years' Experimental Writing in America. New York: New Directions, 1947.

    pp. 250–258: The Place of Death; A Camp in the Prussian Forest; Burning the Letters; Siegfried; Pilots, Man Your Planes.

To Be an American, by William R. Wood and others. New York: J. B. Lippincott, 1957. (Reading for Life Series).

    pp. 54–55, For an Emigrant

Twentieth Century Poetry in English, Contemporary Recordings of the Poets Reading Their Own Poems, The Library of Congress, Music Division. Washington, D. C.: Library of Congress, 1949.

    Album V. P 24 A and B, has reading of 'Lady Bates' and 'Stalag Luft' by Randall Jarrell and text of poems on separate sheet.

transition workshop, ed. by Eugene Jolas. New York: Vanguard, 1949.

    pp. 235–236: Because of Me, Because of You; Enormous love, it's no good asking.

Understanding Poetry, an Anthology for College Students, ed. by Cleanth Brooks and Robert Penn Warren. New York: Henry Holt and Company, 1952. Revised, complete ed.

    p. 221: The Death of the Ball Turret Gunner; pp. 456–457: Losses.

A Vanderbilt Miscellany, 1919–1944, ed. by Richmond Croom Beatty. Nashville: Vanderbilt University Press, 1944.

    pp. 356–361: The Head of Wisdom; For an Emigrant; (pp. 390–391: Notes on the author).

War and the Poet, ed. by Richard Eberhart and Selden Rodman. New York: Devin-Adair, 1945.

p. 200: The Death of the Ball Turret Gunner.

War Poets, an Anthology of the War Poetry of the 20th Century, ed. with an introduction by Oscar Williams. New York: John Day Company, 1945.

pp. 157–163: The Emancipators; The Death of the Ball Turret Gunner; Prisoners; 2nd Air Force; An Officers' Prison Camp Seen from a Troop-Train; The Soldier Walks Under the Trees of the University; Soldier (T. P.); Losses.

Writing from Experience, by Raymond C. Palmer, James A. Lowrie, John F. Speer. Ames, Iowa: Iowa State College Press, 1957.

pp. 78–89: The Schools of Yesteryear.

III. Poems by Randall Jarrell: An Index by Title
and First Line When No Title

'Above the waters in their toil'
   American Review, 3:230, May 1934.
ABSENT WITH OFFICIAL LEAVE
   Poetry, 62:262, Aug. 1943.
   Little Friend, Little Friend, 1945, pp. 33-34.
   Selected Poems, 1955, pp. 165-166.
Aesthetic Theories, see ESTHETIC THEORIES
AFTERWARDS I, II, III, & IV (Four adaptations from Corbière's
      Rondels pour après)
   Poetry, 72:299-301, Sept. 1948.
   The Seven-League Crutches, 1951, pp. 54-56.
   Selected Poems, 1955, pp. 127-130.
AGING
   Poetry, 84:315, Sept. 1954.
ALL OR NONE
   Kenyon Review, 13:204, Spring 1951.
'And did she dwell in innocence and joy'
   Southern Review, 1:84-85, Spring 1935.
THE ANGELS AT HAMBURG
   Poetry, 64:267-268, Aug. 1944.
   Little Friend, Little Friend, 1945, pp. 36-37.
   Selected Poems, 1955, pp. 185-186.
THE AUTOMATON
   Southern Review, 3:392-393, Autumn 1937.
   Five Young American Poets, 1940, pp. 100-101.
   Blood for a Stranger, 1942, pp. 46-47.
THE BAD MUSIC
   Five Young American Poets, 1940, pp. 114-115.
   Blood for a Stranger, 1942, pp. 28-29.
BECAUSE OF ME, BECAUSE OF YOU
   transition, 26:15, Winter 1937.
   Five Young American Poets, 1940, p. 113.
   Blood for a Stranger, 1942, p. 27.
   transition workshop, ed. by E. Jolas, 1949, p. 235.

LA BELLE AU BOIS DORMANT*
>   *Sewanee Review*, 57:656, Autumn 1949.
>   *The Seven-League Crutches*, 1951, p. 77.
>   *Selected Poems*, 1955, pp. 121–122.

THE BLACK SWAN
>   *Kenyon Review*, 13:206, Spring 1951.
>   *The Seven-League Crutches*, 1951, p. 50.
>   *Borestone Mountain Poetry Award*, 1952, p. 4.
>   *Selected Poems*, 1955, p. 45.
>   *Fifteen Modern American Poets*, ed. G. P. Elliott, 1956, p. 47.

THE BLIND SHEEP
>   *New Yorker*, 17:47, Dec. 13, 1941.
>   *Blood for a Stranger*, 1942, p. 30.
>   *Selected Poems*, 1955, p. 91.

Bombers (title of a section of poems)
>   *Selected Poems*, 1955, pp. 135–144.

THE BOYG, PEER GYNT, THE ONE ONLY ONE
>   *Partisan Review*, 11:98–99, Winter 1944.
>   *Little Friend, Little Friend*, 1945, p. 40.
>   *Selected Poems*, 1955, p. 106.

THE BREATH OF NIGHT*
>   *Kenyon Review*, 9:507, Autumn 1947.
>   *Losses*, 1948, p. 30.
>   *N. Y. Times Book Review*, Sect. VII:2, April 4, 1948.
>   *Selected Poems*, 1955, p. 126.
>   *N. Y. Times Book Review*, Sect. VII:2, March 13, 1955.
>   *Criterion Book of Modern American Verse*, ed. by W. H. Auden, 1956, pp. 276–277.

THE BRONZE DAVID OF DONATELLO*
>   *Art News*, 56(no. 6):36–37, Oct. 1957. Illus.

BURNING THE LETTERS
>   *Nation*, 161:372, 374, Oct. 13, 1945.
>   *Spearhead*, 1947, pp. 252–254.
>   *Losses*, 1948, pp. 27–29.
>   *Mid-Century American Poets*, ed. J. Ciardi, 1950, pp. 194–196.
>   *Modern American Poetry*, ed. L. Untermeyer, 1950, pp. 681–682.
>   *Selected Poems*, 1955, pp. 151–153.
>   *Modern American . . . Poetry*, ed. L. Untermeyer, 1955, rev.

shorter ed., p. 375.
An Approach to Literature, by Brooks, Purser, and Warren, 1952, pp. 365–367.

A CAMP IN THE PRUSSIAN FOREST*
Nation, 162:756, June 22, 1946.
Horizon, 16:156–157, Sept. 1947.
Spearhead, 1947, pp. 251–252.
Losses, 1948, pp. 7–8.
Modern American Poetry, ed. L. Untermeyer, 1950, p. 678.
Mid-Century American Poets, ed. J. Ciardi, 1950, pp. 185–186.
Selected Poems, 1955, pp. 161–162.

Camps and Field (title of a section of poems)
Selected Poems, 1955, pp. 163–172.

THE CARNEGIE LIBRARY, JUVENILE DIVISION
Kenyon Review, 6:64–65, Winter 1944.
Little Friend, Little Friend, 1945, pp. 23–24.
Selected Poems, 1955, pp. 89–90.

The Carriers (title of a section of poems)
Selected Poems, 1955, pp. 145–153.

CHARLES DODGSON'S SONG
Poetry, 77:149–150, Dec. 1950.

CHE FARO SENZA EURIDICE
Five Young American Poets, 1940, p. 119.
Blood for a Stranger, 1942, pp. 81–82.

THE CHILD, see Part VI, Translation of Rilke
The Child of Courts, see THE PRINCE
CHILDHOOD, see Part VI, Translation of Rilke

Children (title of a section of poems)
The Seven-League Crutches, 1951, pp. 49–69.

Children and Civilians (title of a section of poems)
Selected Poems, 1955, pp. 183–190.

CHILDREN SELECTING BOOKS IN A LIBRARY
New Republic, 105:790, Dec. 8, 1941.
Blood for a Stranger, 1942, pp. 15–16.
—(Rewritten)*
New Republic, 132:23, Feb. 21, 1955.
Selected Poems, 1955, pp. 97–98.
N. Y. Times Book Review, Sect. VII:2, April 3, 1955.

N. Y. Times Book Review, Sect. VII:2, June 10, 1956.
THE CHRISTMAS ROSES
New Republic, 105:790, Dec. 8, 1941.
Blood for a Stranger, 1942, pp. 77–78.
CINDERELLA*
Art News (annual Christmas edition), 53:86, Nov. 1954. Illus. by John Graham.
Encounter, 3:23, Aug. 1954.
THE CLOCK IN THE TOWER OF THE CHURCH
Kenyon Review, 9:508–509, Autumn 1947.
COME TO THE STONE . . .
Poetry, 62:264, Aug. 1943.
Little Friend, Little Friend, 1945, p. 31.
Selected Poems, 1955, p. 184.
THE CONTRARY POET, see Part VI, Translation of Corbière
A CONVERSATION WITH THE DEVIL
Poetry, 78:1–6, April 1951.
The Seven-League Crutches, 1951, pp. 43–47.
Botteghe Oscure, 7:240–245, 1951.
Selected Poems, 1955, pp. 18–23.
A COUNTRY LIFE
Losses, 1948, pp. 25–26.
N. Y. Times Book Review, Sect. VII:2, May 2, 1948.
Mid-Century American Poets, ed. J. Ciardi, 1950, pp. 197–198.
Modern American Poetry, ed. L. Untermeyer, 1950, pp. 683–684.
North Carolina Poetry, ed. R. Walser, 1951, pp. 166–167.
Selected Poems, 1955, pp. 8–9.
THE COUNTRY WAS (a parody of Marianne Moore's poetry)
Partisan Review, 9:58–60, Jan.–Feb. 1942.
THE COW WANDERING IN THE BARE FIELD . . .
American Review, 3:230–231, May 1934.
Blood for a Stranger, 1942, p. 39.
THE DEAD
Partisan Review, 13:349–350, Summer 1946.
THE DEAD IN MELANESIA
Partisan Review, 12:309, Summer 1946.
Losses, 1948, p. 22.
Mid-Century American Poets, ed. J. Ciardi, 1950, p. 196.

Selected Poems, 1955, p. 182.
THE DEAD WINGMAN
    Nation, 161:232, Sept. 1945.
    Losses, 1948, p. 6.
    Mid-Century American Poets, ed. J. Ciardi, 1950, pp. 187–188.
    Selected Poems, 1955, p. 150.
THE DEATH OF THE BALL TURRET GUNNER*
    Partisan Review, 12:60, Winter 1945.
    Horizon, 11:224, April 1945.
    Little Friend, Little Friend, 1945, p. 58.
    War Poets, ed. O. Williams, 1945, p. 157.
    War and the Poet, ed. Eberhart and Rodman, 1945, p. 200.
    Mid-Century American Poets, ed. J. Ciardi, 1950, p. 198.
    Oxford Book of American Verse . . ., chosen by F. O. Mathiessen, 1950, no. 562, p. 1091.
    Modern American Poetry, ed. L. Untermeyer, 1950, p. 681.
    Understanding Poetry, ed. Brooks and Warren, 1952, p. 221.
    The New Partisan Reader, 1953, p. 166.
    Golden Horizon, ed. C. Connolly, 1953, p. 100.
    Penguin Book of Modern American Verse, selected by G. Moore, 1954, p. 269.
    Selected Poems, 1955, p. 137.
    American Treasury, ed. C. Fadiman, 1955, p. 617.
    Fifteen Modern American Poets, ed. G. P. Elliott, 1956, p. 56.
    The Sound of Wings, ed. Roberts and Briand, 1956, p. 201.
The Death of the Gods, see 1945: THE DEATH OF THE GODS
A DESCRIPTION OF SOME CONFEDERATE SOLDIERS
    Southern Review, 2:374–375, Autumn 1936.
    Five Young American Poets, 1940, pp. 98–99.
    Blood for a Stranger, 1942, pp. 61–62.
DEUTSCH DURCH FREUD
    Poetry, 77:150–153, Dec. 1950.
A DIALOGUE BETWEEN SOUL AND BODY
    Southern Review, 3:398–399, Autumn 1937.
THE DIFFICULT RESOLUTION
    New Republic, 105:790–791, Dec. 8, 1941.
    New Poems, 1942, ed. O. Williams, 1942, pp. 120–122.
    Little Friend, Little Friend, 1945, pp. 41–43.

THE DREAM OF WAKING*
    Poetry, 66:118–119, June 1945.
    Little Friend, Little Friend, 1945, p. 17.
DUMMIES
    Southern Review, 3:396, Autumn 1937.
    Blood for a Stranger, 1942, p. 57.
Dream-Work (title of a section of poems)
    Selected Poems, 1955, pp. 43–54.
EIGHTH AIR FORCE
    Quarterly Review of Literature, 4(no. 1):20, 1947.
    Losses, 1948, p. 20.
    Mid-Century American Poets, ed. J. Ciardi, 1950, p. 188.
    An Approach to Literature, ed. Brooks, Purser, and Warren, 1952, pp. 397–399.
    Selected Poems, 1955, pp. 135–136.
    Reading Modern Poetry, ed. Engle and Carrier, 1955, p. 223.
EINE KLEINE NACHTMUSIK
    Five Young American Poets, 1940, pp. 110–111.
THE EMANCIPATORS
    Poetry, 62:264–265, August 1943.
    Little Friend, Little Friend, 1945, p. 14.
    War Poets, ed. O. Williams, 1945, p. 157.
    Selected Poems, 1955, p. 110.
THE END OF THE RAINBOW*
    Kenyon Review, 16:600–610, Autumn 1954.
AN ENGLISH GARDEN IN AUSTRIA
    Poetry, 75:311–317, March 1950.
    The Seven-League Crutches, 1951, pp. 18–21.
    Selected Poems, 1955, pp. 59–62.
'Enormous love, it's no good asking'
    transition, 26:15–16, Winter 1937.
    transition workshop, ed. E. Jolas, 1949, pp. 235–236.
AN ESSAY ON THE HUMAN WILL
    Southern Review, 7:108–109, Summer 1941.
    Blood for a Stranger, 1942, pp. 58–59.
ESTHETIC THEORIES: ART AS EXPRESSION
    Poetry, 60:72–73, May 1942.
    Blood for a Stranger, 1942, pp. 55–56.

Europe (title of a section of poems)
> *The Seven-League Crutches*, 1951, pp. 7–47.

EVENING, see Part VI, Translation of Rilke

THE FACE
> *Poetry*, 77:147–148, Dec. 1950.
> *The Seven-League Crutches*, 1951, p. 22.
> *Selected Poems*, 1955, pp. 12–13.

'Falling in love is never as simple'
> *Southern Review*, 3:396, Autumn 1937.

FAT, AGING, THE CHILD CLINGING TO HER HAND
> *Southern Review*, 2:376–377, Autumn 1936.
> *Blood for a Stranger*, 1942, pp. 13–14.

FEAR
> *American Review*, 3:228–229, May 1934.
> *Blood for a Stranger*, 1942 (with changes).

A FIELD HOSPITAL
> *Nation*, 164:714, June 14, 1947.
> *Losses*, 1948, p. 34.
> *Selected Poems*, 1955, p. 193.

FOR AN EMIGRANT
> *Kenyon Review*, 2:190–194, Spring 1940.
> *Five Young American Poets*, 1940, pp. 120–123.
> *Blood for a Stranger*, 1942, pp. 18–22.
> *A Vanderbilt Miscellany*, ed. R. C. Beatty, 1944, pp. 358–361.
> *Oxford Book of American Verse* . . ., chosen by F. O. Mathiessen, 1950, no. 558, pp. 1084–1088.
> *The Literature of the South*, ed. R. C. Beatty and others, 1952, pp. 812–815.
> *Selected Poems*, 1955 (first part of poem with some changes under title of 'To the New World'), pp. 70–71.
> *To Be an American*, ed. W. R. Wood, 1957, pp. 54–55.

FOR THE MADRID ROAD
> *Five Young American Poets*, 1940, p. 84 (facsimile), p. 118.
> *Blood for a Stranger*, 1942, p. 45.

THE FORSAKEN GIRL, see Part VI, Translation of Mörike

A FRONT
> *Poetry*, 64:265–266, Aug. 1944.
> *Little Friend, Little Friend*, 1945, p. 27.

Selected Poems, 1955, p. 167.
A GAME AT SALZBURG
   Nation, 168:20, Jan. 1, 1949.
   Mid-Century American Poets, ed. J. Ciardi, 1950, pp. 191–192.
   The Seven-League Crutches, 1951, pp. 9–10.
   Selected Poems, 1955, pp. 57–58.
THE GERMANS ARE LUNATICS
   Kenyon Review, 7:443, Summer 1945.
A GHOST, A REAL GHOST
   Kenyon Review, 7:441–442, Summer 1945.
A GHOST STORY
   Quarterly Review of Literature, 4:20–21, 1947.
THE GIRL DREAMS THAT SHE IS GISELLE
   Nation, 168:664, June 11, 1949.
A GIRL IN A LIBRARY
   Poetry, 78:7–11, April 1951.
   The Seven-League Crutches, 1951, pp. 71–74.
   Botteghe Oscure, 7:237–240, 1951.
   Penguin Book of Modern American Verse, selected by G. Moore, 1954, pp. 271–274.
   Selected Poems, 1955, pp. 3–7.
   Pine Needles, 1956 (annual publication of the Students of Woman's College of the University of North Carolina, Greensboro, N. C.), p. 11. Illus.
   Fifteen Modern American Poets, ed. G. P. Elliott, 1956, p. 42.
GOOD-BYE, WENDOVER: GOOD-BYE, MOUNTAIN HOME
   Poetry, 74:137, June 1949.
   The Seven-League Crutches, 1951, p. 82.
   Selected Poems, 1955, p. 198.
The Graves in the Forest (title of a section of poems)
   Selected Poems, 1955, pp. 121–132.
THE GREAT NIGHT, see Part VI, Translation of Rilke
THE GROWNUP, see Part VI, Translation of Rilke
GUNNER
   Poetry, 66:119–120, June 1945.
   Little Friend, Little Friend, 1945, p. 29.
   N. Y. Times Book Review, Sect. VII:2, Oct. 13, 1946.

Selected Poems, 1955, p. 197.
THE HANGED MAN ON THE GALLOWS . . .
Southern Review, 3:395, Autumn 1937.
Blood for a Stranger, 1942, p. 36.
THE HEAD OF WISDOM
Atlantic Monthly, 168:456–457, Oct. 1941.
American Anthology, ed. T. Boggs, 1942, pp. 49–50.
Blood for a Stranger, 1942, pp. 65–66.
A Vanderbilt Miscellany, ed. R. C. Beatty, 1944, pp. 356–357.
The Literature of the South, ed. R. C. Beatty and others, 1952, pp. 811–812.
HOHENSALZBURG: FANTASTIC VARIATIONS ON A THEME OF ROMANTIC CHARACTER*
Poetry, 74:1–7, April 1949.
The Seven-League Crutches, 1951, pp. 12–17.
Selected Poems, 1955, pp. 76–81.
HOPE
Nation, 167:431, Oct. 16, 1948.
Modern American Poetry . . ., ed. L. Untermeyer, 1950, p. 685.
The Seven-League Crutches, 1951, pp. 80–81.
N. Y. Times Book Review, Sect. VII:2, Sept. 7, 1952.
Selected Poems, 1955, pp. 101–102.
Modern American . . . Poetry, ed. L. Untermeyer, 1955, rev. shorter ed., p. 377.
Hostages, see OVERTURE: THE HOSTAGES
THE ICEBERG
Southern Review, 7:106–107, Summer 1941.
Blood for a Stranger, 1942, pp. 25–26.
IN THE CAMP THERE WAS ONE ALIVE
Nation, 165:477, Nov. 1, 1947.
Losses, 1948, pp. 38–39.
IN THE WARD: THE SACRED WOOD
Nation, 162:472, April 20, 1946.
Losses, 1948, pp. 51–52.
Selected Poems, 1955, pp. 53–54.
IN THOSE DAYS
Ladies' Home Journal, 70:90, Jan. 1953.
THE INDIAN

Southern Review, 2:375, Autumn 1936.
AN INDIAN MARKET IN MEXICO
Arizona Quarterly, 1:19, Spring 1945.
THE ISLAND
Partisan Review, 16:483–484, May 1949.
The Seven-League Crutches, 1951, pp. 78–79.
Selected Poems, 1955, pp. 51–52.
THE ISLANDS
View (New York City), 3:22, April 1943.
JACK
Blood for a Stranger, 1942, p. 54.
JAMESTOWN*
Virginia Quarterly Review, 33:512–513, Autumn 1957.
JANUARY 1938
Southern Review, 7:107–108, Summer 1941.
JEROME* (unpublished)
JEWS AT HAIFA*
Partisan Review, 14:295–296, May–June 1947.
Losses, 1948, pp. 32–33.
Modern American Poetry, ed. L. Untermeyer, 1950, p. 683.
The New Partisan Reader, 1953, pp. 164–165.
Selected Poems, 1955, pp. 157–158.
JONAH
Virginia Quarterly Review, 24:214–215, Spring 1948.
The Seven-League Crutches, 1951, pp. 88–89.
Selected Poems, 1955, pp. 94–95.
THE KING'S HUNT
Poetry, 72:296–298, Sept. 1948.
KIRILOV ON A SKYSCRAPER
Southern Review, 2:378, Autumn 1936.
Blood for a Stranger, 1942, p. 49.
THE KNIGHT, DEATH, AND THE DEVIL
Nation, 172:566, June 16, 1951.
The Seven-League Crutches, 1951, pp. 23–24.
Art News, 50(no. 7):36–37, Nov. 1951. Illus.
Penguin Book of Modern American Verse, selected by G. Moore, 1954, pp. 269–270.
Selected Poems, 1955, pp. 10–11.

> *Criterion Book of Modern Verse*, ed. W. H. Auden, 1956, pp. 277–278.

THE LABORATORY
> *Sewanee Review*, 51:253, Spring 1943.

LADY BATES*
> *Nation*, 166:239–240, Feb. 28, 1948.
> *Losses*, 1948, pp. 3–5.
> *Twentieth Century Poetry in English*, Library of Congress Album V. P 24 (recording), 1949.
> *Mid-Century American Poets*, ed. J. Ciardi, 1950, pp. 199–201.
> *North Carolina Poetry . . .*, ed. R. Walser, 1951, p. 163.
> *Selected Poems*, 1955, pp. 14–16.

LAMENT, see Part VI, Translation of Rilke

LAMENT OF THE CHILDREN OF ISRAEL IN ROME, see Part VI, Translation of Gregorovius

THE LEARNERS
> *Poetry*, 66:121–122, June 1945.
> *Little Friend, Little Friend*, 1945, p. 28.

LEAVE*
> *Poetry*, 66:120, June 1945.
> *Little Friend, Little Friend*, 1945, p. 18.
> *Selected Poems*, 1955, p. 169.

THE LINES
> *Partisan Review*, 13:67, Winter 1946.
> *Losses*, 1948, p. 21.
> *Selected Poems*, 1955, p. 192.
> *Criterion Book of Modern American Verse*, ed. W. H. Auden, 1956, p. 276.

A LITTLE POEM
> *Five Young American Poets*, 1940, pp. 116–117.
> *Blood for a Stranger*, 1942, pp. 11–12.

Lives (title of a section of poems)
> *Selected Poems*, 1955, pp. 3–42.

LONDON
> *New Republic*, 104:574, April 21, 1941.
> *Blood for a Stranger*, 1945, p. 4.

THE LONELY MAN
> *Poetry*, 84:311–312, Sept. 1954.

Encounter, 3:22, Aug. 1954.
THE LONG VACATION (see also THE UTOPIAN JOURNEY
   for rewritten version)
   Kenyon Review, 4:45–46, Winter 1942.
   Blood for a Stranger, 1942, p. 74.
   New Poems, 1942, ed. O. Williams, 1942, pp. 119–120.
'Looking back in my mind I can see'
   Southern Review, 1:85–86, Spring 1935.
LOSS
   Kenyon Review, 7:442, Summer 1945 (with title, 'Losses').
   Losses, 1948, p. 50.
   Selected Poems, 1955, p. 125.
   Fifteen Modern American Poets, ed. G. P. Elliott, 1956, p. 56.
LOSSES
   Poetry, 64:266–267, Aug. 1944.
   Little Friend, Little Friend, 1945, pp. 15–16.
   Oxford Book of American Verse . . ., chosen by F. O. Matthiessen, 1950, no. 563, pp. 1091–1092.
   War Poets, ed. O. Williams, 1945, p. 163.
   Understanding Poetry, ed. Brooks and Warren, 1952, p. 456.
   Selected Poems, 1955, pp. 138–139.
   Anthologie de la Poésie Américaine, ed. A. Bosquet, 1956, pp. 240–241.
THE LOST LOVE
   Atlantic Monthly, 169:493, April 1942.
   Blood for a Stranger, 1942, p. 5.
LOVE, IN ITS SEPARATE BEING . . .
   Southern Review, 3:394–395, Autumn 1937.
   Five Young American Poets, 1940, p. 93.
   Blood for a Stranger, 1942, pp. 34–35.
A LULLABY
   Poetry, 64:265, Aug. 1944.
   Little Friend, Little Friend, 1945, p. 49.
   Selected Poems, 1955, p. 163.
   Fifteen Modern American Poets, ed. G. P. Elliott, p. 57.
THE MACHINE-GUN
   Southern Review, 3:399, Autumn 1937.
   Five Young American Poets, 1940, p. 109.

> *Blood for a Stranger*, 1942, p. 70.

THE MÄRCHEN*
> *Sewanee Review*, 54:269–272, Spring 1946.
> *A Southern Vanguard*, ed. A. Tate, 1947, pp. 153–155.
> *Losses*, 1948, pp. 41–44.
> *Selected Poems*, 1955, pp. 72–75.
> *Fifteen Modern American Poets*, ed. G. P. Elliott, 1956, p. 49.

MAIL CALL
> *Poetry*, 66:119, June 1945.
> *Little Friend, Little Friend*, 1945, p. 35.
> *N. Y. Times Book Review*, Sect. VII:2, Nov. 25, 1945.
> *Selected Poems*, 1955, p. 164.

MAN
> *Poetry*, 60:74-75, May 1942

'A man sick with whirling', see 1789–1939

'The man with the axe stands profound and termless'
> *American Review*, 3:229–230, May 1934.

THE MEMOIRS OF GLÜCKEL OF HAMELN
> *Blood for a Stranger*, 1942, pp. 71–72.

—(Rewritten)*
> *Selected Poems*, 1955, pp. 68–69.

THE METAMORPHOSES
> *Partisan Review*, 11:434, Fall 1944.
> *Little Friend, Little Friend*, 1945, p. 32.
> *Partisan Reader*, 1934–44, 1946, p. 283.
> *Selected Poems*, 1955, p. 188.
> *Fifteen Modern American Poets*, ed. G. P. Elliott, 1956, p. 60.

THE METEORITE
> *Poetry*, 84:313, Sept. 1954.

THE MILLER
> *Arizona Quarterly*, 1:91, Spring 1945.

MONEY*
> *Partisan Review*, 15:45, Jan. 1948.
> *Losses*, 1948, pp. 9–11.
> *Selected Poems*, 1955, pp. 107–109.

MOTHER, SAID THE CHILD
> *Partisan Review*, 11:434, Fall 1944.
> *Little Friend, Little Friend*, 1945, p. 22.

MOVING*
>   *Losses*, 1948, pp. 48-49.
>   *Selected Poems*, 1955, pp. 83-85.

NESTUS GURLEY*
>   *Virginia Quarterly Review*, 32:201-203, Spring 1956 (Emily Clark Balch Prize Winners).
>   *High Life* (Senior High School, Greensboro, N. C.), 32(no. 15):2, May 11, 1956.

NEW GEORGIA
>   *Nation*, 162:263, March 2, 1946.
>   *Losses*, 1948, p. 36.
>   *Selected Poems*, 1955, p. 176.

NEWS
>   *Sewanee Review*, 53:429, Summer 1945.

THE NIGHT BEFORE THE NIGHT BEFORE CHRISTMAS
>   *Kenyon Review*, 11:31-42, Winter 1949.
>   *The Seven-League Crutches*, 1951, pp. 57-69.
>   *Selected Poems*, 1955, pp. 30-42.

1945: THE DEATH OF THE GODS
>   *Nation*, 162:402, April 6, 1946.
>   *Losses*, 1948, p. 47.
>   *Selected Poems*, 1955, p. 178.

1914 (a prose poem)
>   *Partisan Review*, 12:178-180, Spring 1945.
>   *Little Friend, Little Friend*, 1945, pp. 44-46.
>   *Selected Poems*, 1955, pp. 194-196.

1938: TALES FROM THE VIENNA WOODS
>   *Blood for a Stranger*, 1942, p. 10.

1938: THE SPRING DANCES
>   *Southern Review*, 4:580, Winter 1939.
>   *Blood for a Stranger*, 1942, p. 67.

90 NORTH
>   *New Republic*, 104:575, April 21, 1941.
>   *Blood for a Stranger*, 1942, pp. 6-7.
>   *New Poems, 1942*, ed. O. Williams, 1942, pp. 117-118, with title 'A Poem'.
>   *Horizon*, 9:88, Feb. 1944.
>   *Selected Poems*, 1955, pp. 103-104.

> *Modern American . . . Poetry*, ed. L. Untermeyer, 1955, rev. shorter ed., p. 379.
> *Fifteen Modern American Poets*, ed. G. P. Elliott, 1956, p. 55.

NOLLEKENS*
> *Virginia Quarterly Review*, 25:544–546, Autumn 1949.
> *The Seven-League Crutches*, 1951, pp. 25–27.
> *Selected Poems*, 1955, pp. 24–26.

THE NOVEMBER GHOSTS
> *Sewanee Review*, 51:252, Spring 1943.

A NURSERY RHYME
> *Partisan Review*, 7:19–20, Jan.–Feb., 1940.
> *Partisan Reader*, 1934–44, 1946, pp. 239–240.

O MY NAME IT IS SAM HALL
> *Nation*, 162:76, Jan. 19, 1946 (title begins 'Oh, . . .').
> *Losses*, 1948, p. 19.
> *Selected Poems*, 1955, p. 160.

'O the dummies in the windows!', see DUMMIES

'O weary mariners, here shaded, fed'
> *American Review*, 3:299, May 1934.

AN OFFICERS' PRISON CAMP SEEN FROM A TROOP TRAIN
> *Partisan Review*, 11:432–433, Fall 1944.
> *Little Friend, Little Friend*, 1945, pp. 53–54.
> *War Poets*, ed. O. Williams, 1945, p. 160.

OLD POEMS
> *Southern Review*, 2:377, Autumn 1936.

THE OLIVE GARDEN, see Part VI,. Translation of Rilke

AN OLD SONG
> *Southern Review*, 2:379, Autumn 1936.

ON THE RAILWAY PLATFORM
> *Southern Review*, 4:574–575, Winter 1939.
> *Five Young American Poets*, 1940, p. 91.
> *Blood for a Stranger*, 1942, p. 3.

Once Upon a Time (title of a section of poems)
> *The Seven-League Crutches*, 1951, pp. 71–94.
> *Selected Poems*, 1955, pp. 83–98 (with different selection of poems).

ORESTES AT TAURIS
>   *Kenyon Review*, 5:1–11, Winter 1943. (At head of title: 'Pictures from a World').
>   *New Poems, 1943*, ed. O. Williams, pp. 109–121.
>   *Losses*, 1948, pp. 53–63.

THE ORIENT EXPRESS
>   *Nation*, 170:475, May 20, 1950.
>   *The Seven-League Crutches*, 1951, pp. 7–8.
>   *N. Y. Times Book Review*, Sect. VII:2, June 15, 1952.
>   *Selected Poems*, 1955, pp. 55–56.
>   *Fifteen Modern American Poets*, ed. G. P. Elliott, 1956, p. 48.

OVER THE FLORID CAPITALS . . .
>   *Southern Review*, 4:575, Winter 1939.
>   *Blood for a Stranger*, 1942, p. 48.

OVERTURE: THE HOSTAGES*
>   *Kenyon Review*, 9:509, Autumn 1947.

A PERFECTLY FREE ASSOCIATION
>   *Nation*, 168:503, April 30, 1949.

A PICTURE IN THE PAPER
>   *Southern Review*, 4:576–577, Winter 1939.
>   *Blood for a Stranger*, 1942, pp. 37–38.
>   *New Poems, 1942*, ed. O. Williams, 1942, pp. 116–117 (with title 'A Poem').

Pictures from a World, see ORESTES AT TAURIS

A PILOT FROM THE CARRIER*
>   *Poetry*, 66:117–118, June 1945.
>   *Little Friend, Little Friend*, 1945, p. 13.
>   *Modern Poetry*, ed. Friar and Brinnin, 1951, p. 385.
>   *Selected Poems*, 1955, p. 145.

PILOTS, MAN YOUR PLANES
>   *Nation*, 161:581, Dec. 1, 1945.
>   *Spearhead*, 1947, pp. 256–258.
>   *Losses*, 1948, pp. 12–15.
>   *Modern American Poetry*, ed. L. Untermeyer, 1950, pp. 679–680.
>   *Selected Poems*, 1955, pp. 146–149.
>   *Modern American . . . Poetry*, ed. L. Untermeyer, 1955, rev. shorter ed., p. 380.

THE PLACE OF DEATH
  Nation, 163:650, Dec. 7, 1946.
  Spearhead, 1947, pp. 250–251.
  Losses, 1948, pp. 17–18.
  American Sampler, ed. F. C. Rosenberger, 1951, pp. 49–50.
  Selected Poems, 1955, pp. 131–132.
A Poem: 'There I was, here I am: a foot in air', see A PICTURE IN THE PAPER
A POEM FOR SOMEONE KILLED IN SPAIN
  Five Young American Poets, 1940, p. 105.
  Blood for a Stranger, 1942, p. 17.
LE POÈTE CONTUMACE, see Part VI, Translation of Corbière
PORT OF EMBARKATION
  Poetry, 62:263, August 1943.
  Little Friend, Little Friend, 1945, p. 30.
  Mid-Century American Poets, ed. J. Ciardi, 1950, p. 187.
  Selected Poems, 1955, p. 191.
THE PRINCE*
  Kenyon Review, 9:510, Autumn 1947 (with title, 'The Child of Courts').
  Losses, 1948 (with title, 'The Child of Courts'), p. 45.
  Selected Poems, 1955, p. 88.
THE PRINCESS WAKES IN THE WOOD
  Poetry, 77:148–149, Dec. 1950.
PRISONERS
  Partisan Review, 11:433, Fall 1944.
  Little Friend, Little Friend, 1945, p. 52.
  War Poets, ed. O. Williams, 1945, p. 158.
  Oxford Book of American Verse . . ., chosen by F. O. Matthiessen, 1950, no. 561, pp. 1090–1091.
  Selected Poems, 1955, p. 159.
Prisoners (also title of a section of poems)
  Selected Poems, 1955, pp. 155–162.
PROTOCOLS
  Poetry, 66:121, June 1945.
  Little Friend, Little Friend, 1945, p. 38.
  Selected Poems, 1955, p. 187.

A QUILT-PATTERN
> *Virginia Quarterly Review*, 26:219–221, Spring 1950.
> *The Seven-League Crutches*, 1951, pp. 51–53.
> *Selected Poems*, 1955, pp. 48–50.

The Rage for the Lost Penny (title of the section of this book devoted to Randall Jarrell)
> *Five Young American Poets*, 1940, pp. 81–123.

THE RANGE IN THE DESERT
> *Virginia Quarterly Review*, 23:231, Spring 1947.
> *Losses*, 1948, p. 37.
> *Selected Poems*, 1955, p. 170.

REQUIEM FOR THE DEATH OF A BOY, see Part VI, Translation of Rilke

A RHAPSODY ON IRISH THEMES*
> *The Seven-League Crutches*, 1951, pp. 37–40.
> *Selected Poems*, 1955, pp. 64–67.

THE REFUGEES
> *Partisan Review*, 7:20–21, Jan.–Feb. 1940.
> *Five Young American Poets*, 1940, p. 106.
> *Blood for a Stranger*, 1942, p. 33.
> *N. Y. Times Book Review*, Sect. VI:8, Nov. 1, 1942.
> *Modern American Poetry . . .*, ed. L. Untermeyer, 1950, pp. 685–686.
> *Modern American . . . Poetry*, ed. L. Untermeyer, 1955, rev. shorter ed., p. 378.

THE RISING SUN*
> *Kenyon Review*, 9:260–261, Spring 1947.
> *Horizon*, 16:157–158, Sept. 1947.
> *Losses*, 1948, pp. 23–24.
> *Selected Poems*, 1955, pp. 173–175.

The Sacred Wood, see IN THE WARD: THE SACRED WOOD

SCHERZO
> *Partisan Review*, 11:99, Winter 1944.

SEARS ROEBUCK
> *Nation*, 165:506, Nov. 8, 1947.
> *Losses*, 1948, p. 31.
> *Selected Poems*, 1955, p. 99.

2ND AIR FORCE
>   *Nation*, 159:526, Oct. 28, 1944.
>   *Little Friend, Little Friend*, 1945, p. 11–12.
>   *War Poets*, ed. O. Williams, 1945, pp. 158–159.
>   *Selected Poems*, 1955, pp. 171–172.
>   *Fifteen Modern American Poets*, ed. G. P. Elliott, 1956, p. 58.
>   *Sound of Wings*, ed. Roberts and Briand, 1957, pp. 206–207.

THE SEE-ER OF CITIES
>   *Five Young American Poets*, 1940, p. 95.
>   *Blood for a Stranger*, 1942, p. 60.

SEELE IM RAUM
>   *Poetry*, 75:316–319, March 1950.
>   *The Seven-League Crutches*, 1951, pp. 92–94.
>   *Selected Poems*, 1955, pp. 27–29.
>   *Fifteen Modern American Poets*, ed. G. P. Elliott, 1956, p. 45.

1789–1939 (first published without a title)
>   *The Southern Review*, 2:373, Autumn 1936.
>   *Five Young American Poets*, 1940, p. 112.
>   *Blood for a Stranger*, 1942, p. 31.

A SICK CHILD
>   *Nation*, 169:374, Oct. 15, 1949.
>   *The Seven-League Crutches*, 1951, p. 49.
>   *Selected Poems*, 1955, pp. 43–44.
>   *Invitation to Poetry*, by L. Frankenberg, 1956, pp. 251–252.

THE SICK NOUGHT
>   *Poetry*, 64:268–269, Aug. 1944.
>   *Little Friend, Little Friend*, 1945, p. 51.
>   *Oxford Book of American Verse . . .*, chosen by F. O. Matthiessen, 1950, no. 560, pp. 1089–1090.
>   *Selected Poems*, 1955, p. 168.
>   *Anthologie de la Poésie Américaine*, ed. A. Bosquet, 1956, pp. 241–242.

SIEGFRIED*
>   *Nation*, 160:447, April 21, 1945.
>   *Little Friend, Little Friend*, 1945, pp. 19–21.
>   *Spearhead*, 1947, pp. 254–256.
>   *Mid-Century American Poets*, ed. J. Ciardi, 1950, pp. 189–190.
>   *Selected Poems*, 1955, pp. 142–144.

Reading Modern Poetry, ed. Engle and Carrier, 1955, pp. 224–226.

Sound of Wings, ed. Roberts and Briand, 1957, pp. 218–220.

THE SKATERS
Kenyon Review, 4:46–47, Winter 1942.
Blood for a Stranger, 1942, pp. 75–76.
Selected Poems, 1955, pp. 92–93.

THE SLEEPING BEAUTY: VARIATION OF THE PRINCE
Poetry, 72:294–295, Sept. 1948.
The Seven-League Crutches, 1951, pp. 75–76.
Selected Poems, 1955, pp. 86–87.
Fifteen Modern American Poets, ed. G. P. Elliott, 1956, p. 52.

THE SNOW-LEOPARD
Sewanee Review, 53:425, Summer 1945.
Little Friend, Little Friend, 1945, p. 39.
Selected Poems, 1955, p. 105.
Modern Poetry, ed. Friar and Brinnin, 1951, p. 384.

THE SOLDIER
Partisan Review, 11:98, Winter 1944.
Little Friend, Little Friend, 1945, p. 50.

SOLDIER (T. P.)
New Republic, 109:249, Aug. 23, 1943.
Little Friend, Little Friend, 1945, pp. 25–26.
War Poets, ed. O. Williams, 1945, p. 162.

THE SOLDIER WALKS UNDER THE TREES OF THE UNIVERSITY
Nation, 157:186, Aug. 14, 1943.
New Poems, 1944, ed. O. Williams, pp. 237–238.
Little Friend, Little Friend, 1945, pp. 47–48.
War Poets, ed. O. Williams, 1945, p. 161.
Oxford Book of American Verse . . ., chosen by F. O. Matthiessen, 1950, no. 559, pp. 1088–1089.

Soldiers (title of a section of poems)
Selected Poems, 1955, pp. 191–205.

SONG: NOT THERE
Partisan Review, 8:223, May–June 1941.
Blood for a Stranger, 1942, p. 73.
Selected Poems, 1955, p. 96.

SONNETS TO ORPHEUS, see Part VI, Translation of Rilke
A SOUL
>   *Nation*, 168:279, March 5, 1949.
>   *The Seven-League Crutches*, 1951, p. 11.
>   *Selected Poems*, 1955, p. 63.

THE SPHINX'S RIDDLE TO OEDIPUS
>   *Accent*, 13:132, Summer 1953.

STALAG LUFT
>   *Nation*, 164:773, June 28, 1947.
>   *Losses*, 1948, p. 16.
>   *Twentieth Century Poetry in English*, Library of Congress Album V. P 24 B (recording), 1949.
>   *Selected Poems*, 1955, pp. 155–156.

THE STATE
>   *Sewanee Review*, 53:427, Summer 1945.
>   *Little Friend, Little Friend*, 1945, p. 55.
>   *Mid-Century American Poets*, ed. J. Ciardi, 1950, p. 185.
>   *Selected Poems*, 1955, p. 183.

A STORY
>   *Partisan Review*, 6(no. 4):19–20, Summer 1939.
>   *Five Young American Poets*, 1940, pp. 107–108.
>   *Blood for a Stranger*, 1942, pp. 8–9.
>   *Selected Poems*, 1955, pp. 123–124.

THE STREET HAS CHANGED
>   *Sewanee Review*, 53:428, Summer 1945.

THE SUBWAY FROM NEW BRITAIN TO THE BRONX
>   *Nation*, 162:472, April 20, 1946.
>   *Losses*, 1948, p. 46.
>   *Selected Poems*, 1955, p. 177.

THE SURVIVOR AMONG GRAVES
>   *Poetry*, 81:42–44, Oct. 1952.
>   *Borestone Mountain Poetry Awards*, 1953, pp. 43–44.
>   *Antología de la Poesía Norteamericana Contemporánea*, by E. Florit, 1955, pp. 132–134.
>   *Selected Poems*, 1955, pp. 199–201.

TERMS, I & II*
>   *Poetry*, 72:291–294, Sept. 1948.
>   *The Seven-League Crutches*, 1951, pp. 85–87.

Selected Poems, 1955, pp. 203–205.
'There I was, here I am: a foot in air', see A PICTURE IN THE PAPER
TIME AND THE THING-IN-ITSELF IN A TEXTBOOK
Poetry, 60:73–74, May 1942.
TO THE NEW WORLD (not the same poem as FOR AN EMIGRANT)
Sewanee Review, 53:426, Summer 1945.
To the New World (For an emigrant of 1939), see FOR AN EMIGRANT
THE TOWER
Kenyon Review, 13:205, Spring 1951.
The Traders (title of a section of poems)
Selected Poems, 1955, pp. 173–182.
TRANSIENT BARRACKS
Nation, 168:244, Feb. 26, 1949.
The Seven-League Crutches, 1951, pp. 83–84.
Selected Poems, 1955, pp. 140–141.
THE TRAVELLER
Poetry, 77:146–147, Dec. 1950.
THE TRUTH
Sewanee Review, 57:654–655, Autumn 1949.
The Seven-League Crutches, 1951, pp. 28–29.
Selected Poems, 1955, pp. 189–190.
UP IN THE SKY . . .
Southern Review, 4:577, Winter 1939.
Blood for a Stranger, 1942, p. 50.
A UTOPIAN JOURNEY (rewritten from THE LONG VACATION)
Selected Poems, 1955, p. 100.
Fifteen Modern American Poets, ed. G. P. Elliott, 1956, p. 54.
VARIATIONS
New Republic, 104:574–575, April 21, 1941.
Blood for a Stranger, 1942, pp. 79–80.
Mid-Century American Poets, ed. J. Ciardi, 1950, pp. 192–193.
Selected Poems, 1955, pp. 111–112.
THE VENETIAN BLIND
Virginia Quarterly Review, 25:547–548, Autumn 1949.

The Seven-League Crutches, 1951, pp. 90–91.
Selected Poems, 1955, pp. 46–47.
A WAR
Nation, 173:242, Sept. 22, 1951.
Selected Poems, 1955, p. 202.
A WARD IN THE STATES
Virginia Quarterly Review, 23:232, Spring 1947.
Losses, 1948, p. 40.
Selected Poems, 1955, p. 179.
Fifteen Modern American Poets, ed. G. P. Elliott, 1956, p. 60.
WASHING THE CORPSE, see Part VI, Translation of Rilke
THE WAYS AND THE PEOPLES
Poetry, 54:187, July 1939.
Five Young American Poets, 1940, p. 92.
Blood for a Stranger, 1942, p. 32.
'When Achilles fought and fell'
Southern Review, 3:393, Autumn 1937.
WHEN I WAS HOME LAST CHRISTMAS . . .
Losses, 1948, p. 35.
Selected Poems, 1955, p. 17.
WHEN YOU AND I WERE ALL . . .
Southern Review, 4:578–579, Winter 1939.
Five Young American Poets, 1940, pp. 96–97.
Blood for a Stranger, 1942, pp. 40–41.
THE WIDE PROSPECT
Nation, 160:222, Feb. 24, 1945.
Little Friend, Little Friend, 1945, pp. 56–57.
Selected Poems, 1955, pp. 80–81.
The Wide Prospect (also title of a section of poems)
Selected Poems, 1955, pp. 55–79.
WINDOWS*
Poetry, 84:313–314, Sept. 1954.
The Times Literary Supplement: American Writing Today, Sept. 17, 1954, p. XVI.
THE WINTER'S TALE
Kenyon Review, 1:57–59, Winter 1939.
Five Young American Poets, 1940, pp. 102–104.
Blood for a Stranger, 1942, pp. 51–53.

WOMAN
> *Botteghe Oscure*, 11:382–389, 1953.

THE WOMAN AT THE WASHINGTON ZOO* (unpublished)

'The World and Its Life Are Her Dream (title of collection of three poems: London; Variations; and 90 North)
> *New Republic*, 104:574–575, April 21, 1941.

The World is Everything That is the Case (title of a section of poems)
> *Selected Poems*, 1955, pp. 99–119.

ZENO
> *New Republic*, 81:184, Dec. 26, 1934.

IV. Prose by Randall Jarrell: An Index by Title

(See also Part v, Book Reviews)

AGE OF CRITICISM
　Partisan Review, 19:185–201, March 1952.
　Best Articles, 1953, ed. R. Flesch, 1953, pp. 203–222.
　Poetry and the Age, 1953, pp. 70–95.
　American Writers Today, by A. Cowie, 1956, pp. 198–204.
ANSWER TO QUESTIONS
　Mid-Century American Poets, ed. J. Ciardi, 1950, pp. 182–184.
Anthologies, see A VERSE CHRONICLE, VI
Bad Poets, see A VERSE CHRONICLE, VII
Blackmur, R. P., see A VERSE CHRONICLE, V
CHANGES OF ATTITUDE AND RHETORIC IN AUDEN'S POETRY
　Southern Review, 7:326–349, Autumn 1941.
THE COLLECTED POEMS OF WALLACE STEVENS*
　Yale Review, 44:340–353, Spring 1955.
Comfort, Alex, see A VERSE CHRONICLE, II
Constance and the Rosenbaums, see PICTURES FROM AN INSTITUTION, Book IV
CONTEMPORARY POETRY CRITICISM
　New Republic, 105:88–90, July 21, 1941 and 105:43a, Oct. 6, 1941.
Corbière, Tristan, see A VERSE CHRONICLE, III
CRITICAL SCHOLARS (letter)
　New Republic, 105:439, Oct. 6, 1941. (Comments on above letter by David Daiches in *New Republic*, Aug. 18, 1941, p. 223)
cummings, e. e., see REFLECTIONS ON WALLACE STEVENS
De La Mare, Walter, see A VERSE CHRONICLE, I
THE DEVELOPMENT OF YEATS'S SENSE OF REALITY
　Southern Review, 7:653–666, Winter 1941.
END OF THE LINE
　Nation, 154:222, 224, 226, 228, Feb. 21, 1942.
　Literary Opinion in America, ed. M. D. Zabel, rev. ed. 1951, pp. 742–748.

THE FALL OF THE CITY (article on A. MacLeish's *The Fall of the City*)
    Sewanee Review, 51:267–280, April–June 1943.
FREUD TO PAUL, THE STAGES OF AUDEN'S IDEOLOGY*
    Partisan Review, 12:437–457, Fall 1945.
FROM THE KINGDOM OF NECESSITY (review article on *Lord Weary's Castle* by Robert Lowell)
    Nation, 164:74, 76, Jan. 18, 1947.
    Mid-Century American Poets, ed. J. Ciardi, 1950, pp. 158–167 under title of 'Robert Lowell's Poetry'.
    Poetry and the Age, 1953, pp. 208–219.
    Readings for Liberal Education, ed. L. G. Locke and others. Part II, pp. 279–280 under title of 'On Lowell's Where the Rainbow Ends'.
Frost, Robert, see THE OTHER ROBERT FROST and TO THE LAODICEANS
Gertrude and Sidney, see PICTURES FROM AN INSTITUTION, Book v
GO, MAN, GO!
    Mademoiselle, 45:98–99, 140–143, May 1957.
GRAVES AND THE WHITE GODDESS (articles on *Collected Poems* of Robert Graves [Part I], and other new poetry volumes [at end of Part II] by William Carlos Williams, Louis O. Coxe, Robert Conquest, Alan Ross, John Ciardi, Conrad Aiken, Phyllis Deborah Cummins, Adrienne Cecile Rich)
    Yale Review (Part I) 45, no. 2:302–314, Dec. 1955; (Part II) 45, no. 3:467–480, March 1955.
HER SHIELD (essay on Marianne Moore)
    Partisan Review, 19:687–700, Nov. 1952 (with title, 'Thoughts about Marianne Moore').
    Poetry and the Age, 1953, pp. 185–207.
THE HUMBLE ANIMAL (review article on *What Are Years* by Marianne Moore, 1941)
    Kenyon Review, 4:408–411, Autumn 1942.
    Kenyon Critics, ed. J. C. Ransom, 1951, pp. 277–280.
    Poetry and the Age, 1953, pp. 179–184.
THE INTELLECTUAL IN AMERICA
    Mademoiselle, 40:48, pp. 121–123, Jan. 1955.

Essays Today, 2, ed. R. M. Ludwig, 1956, pp. 129–134.
AN INTRODUCTION TO THE SELECTED POEMS OF WILLIAM CARLOS WILLIAMS
Selected Poems, by W. C. Williams. N. Y.: New Directions, 1949, pp. ix–xix.
Poetry and the Age, 1953, pp. 237–249.
Literature in America, ed. P. Rahv, 1957, pp. 342–349.
JOHN RANSOM'S POETRY
Sewanee Review, 56:378–390, Summer 1948.
Poetry and the Age, 1953, pp. 96–111.
THE LITTLE CARS
Vogue, 124:128–129, Sept. 15, 1954. Portrait.
LOVE AND POETRY*
Mademoiselle, 42:123, 223, Feb. 1956. Portrait, p. 98.
Lowell, Robert, see FROM THE KINGDOM OF NECESSITY
Miss Batterson and Benton, see PICTURES FROM AN INSTITUTION, Book III
Moore, Marianne, see HER SHIELD, and THE HUMBLE ANIMAL
MR. JARRELL REPLIES (reply to article 'Poets as Reviewers' by Malcolm Cowley in New Republic, Feb. 24, 1941)
New Republic, 104:374–375, March 17, 1941.
A NOTE ON POETRY
Five Young American Poets, 1940, pp. 85–90.
THE OBSCURITY OF THE POET
Partisan Review, 18:66–81, Jan.–Feb. 1951.
Poetry and the Age, 1953, pp. 3–27.
THE OTHER ROBERT FROST (article on A Masque of Mercy by Robert Frost)
Nation, 165:588, 590–592, Nov. 29, 1947.
Poetry and the Age, 1953, pp. 28–36.
PICTURES FROM AN INSTITUTION, Book I
Kenyon Review, 15:104–126, Winter 1953.
PICTURES FROM AN INSTITUTION, Book III: Miss Batterson and Benton
Kenyon Review, 16:81–123, Winter 1954.
PICTURES FROM AN INSTITUTION, Book IV*: Constance and the Rosenbaums

Accent, 13:227–262, Autumn 1953.
PICTURES FROM AN INSTITUTION, Book v: Gertrude and Sidney
Sewanee Review, 61:633–657, Autumn 1953.
The Best American Short Stories, 1954, ed. M. Foley, 1954, pp. 185–205.
A New Southern Harvest, ed. Warren and Erskine, 1957, pp. 147–164.
PICTURES FROM AN INSTITUTION (epigrams selected from the novel)
Vogue, 123:88–89, 1935, April 15, 1954.
Poets, see Part v, Book Reviews, 1946, THE POET AND HIS PUBLIC
PYLE, ERNIE
Nation, 160:573–576, May 19, 1945.
Ransom, John, see JOHN RANSOM'S POETRY
READING POETRY (a selection from *Poetry and the Age*)
N. Y. Times Book Review, Sect. vii:2, Aug. 23, 1953.
REFLECTIONS ON WALLACE STEVENS
Partisan Review, 18:335–345, May–June 1951.
Poetry and the Age, 1953, pp. 133–148.
The New Partisan Reader, 1953, pp. 408–421 (with title 'Reflections on Wallace Stevens and e. e. cummings'. Part ii on e. e. cummings reprinted in part from review 'The Profession of Poetry' in *Partisan Review*, 17:724–731, Sept.–Oct. 1950).
Rukeyser, Muriel, see A VERSE CHRONICLE, IV
THE SCHOOLS OF YESTERYEAR, A ONE-SIDED DIALOGUE*
New Republic, 135(no. 21):13–17, Nov. 19, 1956.
Writing from Experience, 1957, pp. 78–89.
THE 'SERIOUS' CRITIC (relating to review of Conrad Aiken's poetry)
Nation, 166:670–672, June 12, 1948.
THE SITUATION OF A POET (review article on *Collected Earlier Poems* by William Carlos Williams)
Perspectives U. S. A. (published also in British, French, German, and Italian, no. 1:165–168, Fall 1952 (on p. 189 biographical note and portrait)

Poetry and the Age, 1953, pp. 266–271.
SOME LINES FROM WHITMAN (first appeared under editor's title, 'Walt Whitman: He Had His Nerve')
Kenyon Review, 14:63–79, Winter, 1952.
Perspectives U. S. A. (published also in British, French, German, and Italian), no. 2:61–77, Winter 1953.
Poetry and the Age, 1953, pp. 112–132.
SPEAKING OF BOOKS* (comments by J. Donald Adams on this article, *N. Y. Times Book Review*, Sect. VII:2, Dec. 18, 1955)
N. Y. Times Book Review, Sect. VII:2, July 24, 1955.
Stevens, Wallace, see REFLECTIONS ON WALLACE STEVENS, and THE COLLECTED POEMS OF WALLACE STEVENS
TEXTS FROM HOUSMAN
Kenyon Review, 1:260–271, Summer 1939.
Thoughts about Marianne Moore, see HER SHIELD
Three Books, see A VIEW OF THREE POETS
see also Part V, Book Reviews, Nov. 1951
TO THE LAODICEANS
Kenyon Review, 14:535–561, Autumn 1952.
Poetry and the Age, 1953, pp. 37–69.
Two essays on Marianne Moore, see THE HUMBLE ANIMAL and HER SHIELD
Two Essays on Robert Frost, see THE OTHER FROST and TO THE LAODICEANS
A VERSE CHRONICLE (reviews reprinted from *The Nation* to which Mr. Jarrell has 'added several paragraphs to several')
   I Walter de la Mare. *Nation*, 162:134–136, Feb. 2, 1946.
   II Alex Comfort. *Nation*, 161:741–742, Dec. 29, 1945.
   III Tristan Corbière. *Nation*, 165:424–425, Oct. 18, 1947.
   IV Muriel Rukeyser. *Nation*, 176:512–513, May 8, 1948.
   V R. P. Blackmur. *Nation*, 166:447–448, April 24, 1948.
   VI Anthologies. *Nation*, 162:237–238, Feb. 23, 1946.
   VII Bad Poets. *Nation*, 162:632–634, May 25, 1946.
Poetry and the Age, 1953, pp. 149–178.
A VIEW OF THREE POETS (review of *Ceremony and other Poems* by Richard Wilbur, *The Mills of the Kavanaughs* by Robert Lowell, and *Paterson* by William Carlos Williams)

Partisan Review, 18:691–700, Nov.–Dec. 1951.
Poetry and the Age, 1953 (in chapter entitled, 'Three Books'), pp. 250–265.
Walt Whitman: He Had His Nerve, see SOME LINES FROM WHITMAN
Williams, William Carlos, see AN INTRODUCTION TO THE SELECTED POEMS OF WILLIAM CARLOS WILLIAMS
WRITERS AND CRITICS (a selection from *Poetry and the Age*)
N. Y. Times Book Review, Sect. VII:2, Nov. 22, 1953.

V. Book Reviews by Randall Jarrell: Arranged Chronologically

1935

TEN BOOKS (review of ten new books by the following authors: Ellen Glasgow, Erskine Caldwell, Stark Young, James Hanley, Jule Brousseau, Gale Wilhelm, Tess Slesinger, Willa Cather, Rachel Field, Raymond Holden)
Southern Review, 1:397–410, Autumn 1935.

1939

THE MORALITY OF MR. WINTERS (review of *Maule's Curse* by Yvor Winters)
Kenyon Review, 1:211–215, Spring 1939.
FROM THAT ISLAND (review of *Modern Poetry: A Personal Essay* by Louis MacNeice)
Kenyon Review, 1:468–471, Autumn 1939.

1940

POETRY IN A DRY SEASON (review of poetry by William Bacon Evans, Florence Becker, Walter Roberts, Gordon Fraser, Reual Denny, Archibald MacLeish, Kenneth Patchen, Robert Graves, Muriel Rukeyser, Dylan Thomas, Wystan H. Auden)
Partisan Review, 7:164–167, March–April 1940.
Partisan Reader, 1934–44, 1946, pp. 629–633.
POETS: OLD, NEW AND AGING (review of books by Leonard Bacon, Witter Bynner, Ezra Pound, and Frederic Prokosch)
New Republic, 103:797–800, Dec. 9, 1940.
A JOB LOT OF POETRY (review of poems by Joyce Kilmer, Sydney Salt, J. Calder Joseph, Elder Olson)
New Republic, 103:667–668, Dec. 11, 1940.

1941

KAFKA'S TRAGI-COMEDY (review of *Amerika* by Franz Kafka)
Kenyon Review, 3:116–120, Winter 1941.

THE RHETORICIANS (review of books by Conrad Aiken and Raymond Holder)
New Republic, 104:221–222, Feb. 17, 1941.
NEW YEAR LETTER (review of *The Double Man* by Wystan H. Auden)
Nation, 152:440–441, April 12, 1941.

1942

IN ALL DIRECTIONS (review of *New Directions*, 1941)
Partisan Review, 9:345–347, July–Aug. 1942.
THE HUMBLE ANIMAL (review of *What Are Years* by Marianne Moore)
Kenyon Review, 4:408–411, Autumn 1942.
See also Part IV, 'Prose by Randall Jarrell'.

1945

THESE ARE NOT PSALMS (review of *Poems* by Abraham M. Klein)
Commentary 1(no. 1):88–90, Nov. 1945.
POETRY IN WAR AND PEACE (review of poetry of Marianne Moore, William Carlos Williams, H(ilda) D(oolittle), *Five Young American Poets*, Robert Lowell)
Partisan Review, 12:120–126, Winter 1945.
VERSE CHRONICLE (reviews of *Tribute to the Angels* by H(ilda) D(oolittle) and *The Song of Lazarus* by Alex Comfort)
Nation, 161:741–742, Dec. 29, 1945.
Poetry and the Age, 1953, pp. 154–157 (with title, 'Alex Comfort').

1946

VERSE CHRONICLE (review of *The Burning-Glass* by Walter de la Mare)
Nation, 162:134–136, Feb. 2, 1946.
Reprinted in *Poetry and the Age*, 1953, pp. 149–154 (with title, 'Walter de la Mare').
VERSE CHRONICLE (review of *Selected Poems* of Marsden Hartley and *War and the Poet* by Richard Eberhart and Selden Rodman)
Nation, 162:237–238, Feb. 23, 1946.

Poetry and the Age, 1953, pp.170–176 (with title, 'Anthologies').
VERSE CHRONICLE (review of verse by Oscar Williams, Arnold Stein, Stanton A. Coblentz, Ruth Pitter)
Nation, 162:632–634, May 25, 1946.
Poetry and the Age, 1953, pp. 176–178 (with title, 'Bad Poets').
THE POET AND HIS PUBLIC (review of poetry by Josephine Miles, Adam Drinan, Robert Graves, Denis Devlin, William Carlos Williams, Elizabeth Bishop, and *A Little Treasury of Modern Poetry*)
Partisan Review, 13:488–500, Sept.–Oct. 1946.
Poetry and the Age, 1953, pp. 220–236 (with title 'Poets').

1947

'TENDERNESS AND PASSIVE SADNESS' (review of *Steeple Bush* by Robert Frost)
N. Y. Times Book Review, Sect. VII:4, June 1, 1947.
CORRECTIVE FOR CRITICS (review of *In Defense of Reason* by Yvor Winters)
N. Y. Times Book Review, Sect. VII:14, August 24, 1947.
POEMS BY CORBIÈRE (review of *Poems* by Tristan Corbière, trans. by Walter McElroy)
N. Y. Times Book Review, Sect. VII:5, Sept. 28, 1947.
VERSE CHRONICLE (review of *The Age of Anxiety* by Wystan H. Auden and *Poems* by Tristan Corbière, trans. by Walter McElroy)
Nation, 165:424–425, Oct. 18, 1947.
Poetry and the Age, 1953, pp. 158–166 (with title, 'Tristan Corbière').

1948

VERSE CHRONICLE (review of poetry of Henry Reed, Rolfe Humphries, John Ciardi)
Nation, 166:360–361, March 27, 1948.
VERSE CHRONICLE (review of Richard P. Blackmur's *The Good European*)
Nation, 166:447–448, April 24, 1948.
Poetry and the Age, 1953, pp. 166–170 (with title, 'R. P. Blackmur').

VERSE CHRONICLE (review of poetry by Jean Garrigue, Conrad Aiken, Muriel Rukeyser)
  Nation, 166:512-513, May 8, 1948.
  Poetry and the Age, 1953, pp. 163-166 (with title, 'Muriel Rukeyser')
VERSE CHRONICLE (review of poetry of Karl Shapiro, Bertolt Brecht, John Berryman)
  Nation, 167:80-81, July 17, 1948.

1949

BERNARD H. HAGGIN (review of his *Music in the Nation*)
  Nation, 169:599-600, Dec. 17, 1949.

1950

POETRY, UNLIMITED (review of poetry by Louis Simpson, Elizabeth Coatsworth, Donald F. Drummond, John Williams, Theodore Spencer, Harry Brown, Francis Golffing, José Garcia Villa)
  Partisan Review, 17:189-193, Feb. 1950.
THE PROFESSION OF POETRY (review of poetry by Marshall Schacht, John Frederick Nims, Howard Nemerov, Alfred Hayes, e. e. cummings, Isaac Rosenberg, Wilfred Owen)
  Partisan Review, 17:724-731, Sept.-Oct. 1950.
  New Partisan Reader, 1953, pp. 418-421 (with title 'Reflections on Wallace Stevens and e. e. cummings').

1951

NO LOVE FOR ELIOT (review of *The T. S. Eliot Myth* by Rossell Hope Robbins)
  N. Y. Times Book Review, Sect. VII:36, Nov. 18, 1951.
TO FILL A WILDERNESS (review of *A Dictionary of Americanisms*, ed. Mitford M. Mathews)
  Nation, 173:570, Dec. 29, 1951.
A VIEW OF THREE POETS (review of *Ceremony and other Poems* by Richard Wilbur, *The Mills of the Kavanaughs* by Robert Lowell, and *Paterson* by William Carlos Williams)
  Partisan Review, 18:691-700, Nov.-Dec., 1951.
  Poetry and the Age, 1953 (with title 'Three Books').

1953

ON THE UNDERSIDE OF THE STONE (review of *Brother to Dragons* by Robert Penn Warren)
  N. Y. Times Book Review, Sect. VII:6, Aug. 23, 1953.

MALRAUX'S THUNDER OF SILENCE (review of *The Voices of Silence* by André Malraux)
  Art News, 52(no. 8):24–25, 54, Dec. 1953.

1954

ARISTOTLE ALIVE! (review of *The Language of Criticism and the Structure of Poetry* by Ronald S. Crane)
  Saturday Review of Literature, 37:29, April 3, 1954.

'THE POET'S STORE OF GRAVE AND GAY' (review of *Collected Poems* by James Stephens)
  N. Y. Times Book Review, Sect. VII:5, Aug. 15, 1954.

A POET'S OWN WAY (review of *Poems: 1923–1954* by e. e. cummings)
  N. Y. Times Book Review, Sect. VII:6, Oct. 31, 1954.

THE NEW BOOKS: 'VERY GRACEFUL ARE THE USES OF CULTURE'★ (review of books by John P. Marquand, Arnold Toynbee, Frans G. Bengtsson, Wallace Stevens, Evelyn Waugh, Russell Lynes, Hamilton Basso, Wright Morris, Malcolm Cowley, and others)
  Harper's, 209:94, 96, 98, 100, 102, 104, Nov. 1954.

1955

A LITERARY TORNADO (review of *Selected Poems* by Roy Campbell)
  N. Y. Times Book Review, Sect. VII:4, April 17, 1955.

A MATTER OF OPINION (review of *Predilections* by Marianne Moore)
  N. Y. Times Book Review, Sect. VII:5, May 29, 1955.

A DYLAN THOMAS COLLECTION (review of *Adventures in the Skin Trade* by Dylan Thomas)
  New York Post, June 5, 1955.

RECENT POETRY (review of poetry by Edith Sitwell, James Stephens, Christopher Fry, James Kirkup, Mark Van Doren,

Elder Olson, William H. Matchett, Rolfe Humphries, Constance Carrier, Archibald MacLeish, Wystan H. Auden)
Yale Review, 44:598–608, Summer 1955.
RECENT POETRY* (review of poetry by Isabella Gardner, David Ignatow, Lincoln Fitzell, Howard Nemerov, Ben Belitt, Stephen Spender)
Yale Review, 45:122–132, Sept. 1955.
THE YEAR IN POETRY (review of poetry by Dylan Thomas, Wallace Stevens, Emily Dickinson, Elizabeth Bishop, Robert Graves, Wystan H. Auden, and others)
Harper's, 211:96–101, Oct. 1955.

1956

GRAVES AND THE WHITE GODDESS (review article in two parts essentially on Robert Graves but also short reviews at end on writing of William Carlos Williams, Louis O. Coxe, Robert Conquest, Alan Ross, John Ciardi, Conrad Aiken, Phyllis D. Cummins, Adrienne C. Rich), see Part IV, Prose by Randall Jarrell
WITH BERLIOZ, ONCE UPON A TIME . . . (review of *Evenings with the Orchestra* by Hector Berlioz)
N. Y. Times Book Review, Sect. VII:3, April 15, 1956.
HARMONY, DISCORD AND TASTE (review of *The Listener's Musical Companion* by Bernard H. Haggin)
N. Y. Times Book Review, Sect. VII:7, June 17, 1956.
FIVE POETS (review of poetry by Adrienne C. Rich, Ezra Pound, Rolfe Humphries, Donald Hall, Katherine Hoskins)
Yale Review, 46:100–110, Autumn 1956.
SONGS OF RAPTURE, SONGS OF DEATH (review of *Selected Writings of Jules Laforgue*, ed. and trans. by William J. Smith)
N. Y. Times Book Review, Sect. VII:5, 50, Nov. 25, 1956.

1957

IN PURSUIT OF BEAUTY (review of *A Swinger of Birches: A Portrait of Robert Frost* by Sidney Cox)
N. Y. Times Book Review, Sect. VII:5, March 10, 1957.

VI. Translations by Randall Jarrell: Arranged by Author

Chekov, Anton
    THE THREE SISTERS* (unpublished)
        Mimeographed by the Drama Department at WCUNC for production in 1954.
Corbière, Tristan
    LE POÈTE CONTUMACE
        Poetry (with title, 'The Contrary Poet'), 76:249–256, Aug. 1950.
        The Seven-League Crutches (with title 'The Contrary Poet'), 1951, pp. 30–36.
        Selected Poems, 1955, pp. 113–119.
Gregorovius, Ferdinand
    LAMENT OF THE CHILDREN OF ISRAEL IN ROME
        Commentary, 5:171–172, Feb. 1948.
        The Ghetto and the Jews of Rome. N. Y.: Schocken Books, 1948, pp. 11–16.
Mörike, Eduard Friedrich
    THE FORSAKEN GIRL
        Ladies' Home Journal, 69:101, Sept. 1952.
Rilke, Rainer Maria
    THE CHILD* (unpublished)
    CHILDHOOD* (unpublished)
    EVENING* (unpublished)
    THE GREAT NIGHT* (unpublished)
    THE GROWNUP
        Prairie Schooner, 30:351, Winter 1956.
    LAMENT* (unpublished)
    THE OLIVE GARDEN
        Nation, 167:700, Dec. 18, 1948.
        The Seven-League Crutches, 1951, pp. 41–42.
        N. Y. Times Book Review, Sect. VII:2, Sept. 19, 1954.
    REQUIEM FOR THE DEATH OF A BOY*
        Partisan Review, 20:191–193, March–April, 1953.
    SONNETS TO ORPHEUS* (unpublished)
    WASHING THE CORPSE* (unpublished)

VII. Randall Jarrell: Brief Biographical Notes, Publications, Literary Prizes, and Appointments

1914 Born in Nashville, Tennessee, May 6; son of Owen and Anna Campbell Jarrell.
1915–27 Spent much of childhood in San Francisco, Los Angeles, Long Beach, California.
1928–31 Attended Hume-Fogg High School in Nashville, Tennessee.
1935 Graduated from Vanderbilt University with a B.S. degree.
1935–37 Graduate work at Vanderbilt University.
1936 Received the Southern Review Poetry Prize (*Southern Review*, Autumn, 1936, p. xiii).
1937–39 Instructor in English, Kenyon College.
1939 Received an M.A. degree from Vanderbilt University on submission of thesis: 'Implicit Generalization in Housman'.
1939–42 Instructor in English, University of Texas.
1942 *Blood for a Stranger*, published by Harcourt, Brace.
1942–46 Served in the U. S. Army Air Force. First flew, then washed out, then was Celestial Navigation tower operator chiefly at B29 base in Arizona.
1943 Received the Jeannette Sewell Davis Prize for 'Four Poems', printed in the August issue of *Poetry* (*Poetry*, 63:114, Nov. 1943).
1945 *Little Friend, Little Friend*, published by Dial.
1946 Received the John Peale Bishop Memorial Literary Prize for the poem 'The Märchen', (*Sewanee Review*, announcerment on first page, unnumbered, after cover of the Winte-1946 issue).
Received the John Simon Guggenheim Memorial Foundation Post-Service Fellowship.
1946–47 Taught at Sarah Lawrence College; was literary editor of *The Nation*

1947–58	Associate Professor in English at the Woman's College of the University of North Carolina, with leaves of absence for the periods 1951–53 and 1956–58.
1948	Taught at the Salzburg Seminar in American Civilization during the summer. Received the Levinson Prize (*Poetry*, 73:104, Nov. 1948). *Losses*, published by Harcourt, Brace.
1949–51	Served as Poetry Critic for the *Partisan Review*.
1951	Received award from National Institute of Arts and Letters (*Publishers' Weekly*, 159:1872, May 5, 1951). *The Seven-League Crutches*, published by Harcourt, Brace. Received the Oscar Blumenthal Prize for Poetry (*Poetry*, 79:99, Nov. 1951).
1951–52	Visiting Professor at Princeton University, teaching Seminars in Literary Criticism.
1952	Taught in Indiana University School of Letters, Summer.
1953	Taught in Illinois University, Winter, Second Semester. *Poetry and the Age*, published by Knopf.
1954	*Pictures from an Institution*, published by Knopf. A judge of the Bollingen Award.
1955	A judge of the Bollingen Award. A judge for the Lamont Poetry Selection Contest sponsored by the Academy of American Poets.
1955	A judge of the National Book Award. *Selected Poems*, published by Knopf.
1955–57	Poetry Critic for the *Yale Review*.
1956	Elected to the Board of Chancellors of American Academy of Poets.
1956–58	Consultant in Poetry in English, Library of Congress, for two-year appointment beginning September 1956.
1957	Appointed to the Editorial Board of the *American Scholar*.
1958	Appointed to the Elliston Chair of Poetry at the University of Cincinnati, for six weeks, starting in February. Appointed to the rank of Professor at the Woman's College of the University of North Carolina, effective September.

www.ingramcontent.com/pod-product-compliance
Lightning Source LLC
Chambersburg PA
CBHW031714230426
43668CB00006B/215